AF552542

PROBLEMS OF PRIVATE SCHOOL TEACHERS

By

Dr. Digumarti Bhaskara Rao
M.Sc., M.A., M.A., M.Ed., Ph.D.,
Reader and Research Director
R.V.R. College of Education
Srinivasa Nagar Colony
Guntur–522 006
Andhra Pradesh
India

&

Shaik Abdul Khadar
M.A., M.Ed.,
Principal
Hindi Teacher Training College
Avanigadda
Krishna District
Andhra Pradesh

DISCOVERY PUBLISHING HOUSE
NEW DELHI-110002

First Published – 2004

Reprinted – 2015

ISBN: 978-81-7141-838-1

Problems of Private School Teachers

Published by:

DISCOVERY PUBLISHING HOUSE PVT. LTD.
4383/4B, Ansari Road, Darya Ganj
New Delhi-110 002 (India)
Phone: +91-11-23279245, 43596064-65
Fax: +91-11-23253475
E-mail: discoverypublishinghouse@gmail.com
sales@discoverypublishinggroup.com
web: www.discoverypublishinggroup.com

Printed at:
Infinity Imaging Systems
Delhi

DEDICATED

TO

The Successful School Management

Mr. Veeramachaneni Venkateswara Rao

Mrs. Veeramachaneni Vijaya Lakshmi

Mr. Veeramachaneni Vamsi Krishna

Ravindra Bharathi Public School

Satyanarayanapuram, Vijayawada, A.P.

Preface

The private sector in India is playing a pivotal role in educating the huge population of India. The educational institutions managed by it outnumber the institutions run by the central and state governments. Most of the people and pupils prefer private educational institutions, particularly schools, as they provide quality education.

Several people and personnel feel that the teachers working in private schools face several problems, though they are part and parcel of quality and quantity education, education for all, and conversation of education. Taking this fact into consideration, this small research study has been taken up to assess the level of problems faced by the teachers working in private secondary schools. This study revealed that the private school teachers are facing several problems in varying degrees.

The results of this study will help the planners and administrators in promoting the status of teachers to further enhance the quality of education in school.

Dr. Digumarti Bhaskara Rao

Teacher's Day, 2004

Sai Soudha
D-43, S.V.N. Colony
Guntur–522 006
Andhra Pradesh
India

Contents

Preface

1. **Introduction** 1-12

Importance of Education in Human Life, Secondary Education, Teaching, Teacher, Statement of the Problem, Need of the Study, Objectives of the study, Scope of the Study

2. **Related Literature** 13-26

Secondary Education, Nature of Teaching, Role of the Teacher, Job Satisfaction and Teachers' Problems, Economic Status and Teachers' Problems, Age and Teachers, Problems, Sex and Teachers' Problems, Experience and Teachers' Problems, Language and Non-language Teachers' Problems, Management and Teachers' Problems, Efficiency and Teachers' Problems, Facilities and Teachers' Problems, Marital Status and Teachers' Problems

3. **Design of the Research** 27-36

Operational Definitions of Key Terms, Private Schools, The Teacher, Secondary School Teachers, Secondary School Teachers' Problems, Variables of the Study, Men and Women Teachers, Recognised and Unrecognised School Teachers, Science and Social Studies Teachers, Hypotheses of the Study, Sample of the Study, Tool of the Study, Administration of Tool

4. Analysis of Data **37-40**

Hypothesis 1, Hypothesis 2, Hypothesis 3, Hypothesis 4

5. Summary, Conclusions and Discussions **41-47**

Conclusions and Discussions, Suggestions for Further Research

Bibliography *48*

Additional Reading *51*

Appendix *67*

Index *71*

1

Introduction

Life is a real process and sometimes a mysterious one. Human life is intellectually more powerful than other creatures. Man is superior to other creatures. But his superiority does not depend upon his physical power. Animals like lions, tigers, elephants, bulls, horses, camels and buffaloes are physically much stronger than man. But man has dominated them all by his intellectual power. Intelligence seems to be the last thing in the process of development.

Man is the father of civilization and culture. The progress of civilization and culture depends on man. Education greatly helps both. Man learns something everyday and every moment. His entire life is a continuous process of education. Society produces educated persons in order to pass on civilization and culture to the next generations. So, the education is very important for the progress of both the individual and the society.

The word education has a very wide connotation. It is hard to define. There is no single objective which can cover the whole of life with its various manifestations. Philosophers and thinkers from Socrates to Dewey in the west and Yagnavalka to Gandhi in the east have defined education in accordance with their philosophy of life. With the result, there emerged divergent concepts and definitions of education. The concept of education is like a diamond which appears to be of a different colour when seen from a different angle.

In the ancient period, all the political, economic and social currents emanated from spiritualism. The principle upon which education in the ancient period was founded can be expressed best in the following words, "Learning in India through the ages had been prized and pursued not for its own sake, if we may so put it, but for the sake, and as a part of religion. It was sought as the means of salvation or self-realisation, as the means to the highest end of life". As is the case today, the home is the child's first school. The family is his primary school. He learns many things unconsciously as a part of his growth and development. He acquires the rudiments of social behaviour and the language of society from the home itself.

From the view point of education, India's ancient period has been so glorious and rich that foreign scholars have praised it lavishly. Dr. F.W. Thomas has stated that "Education is no new thing for India. No other country in the world has a more ancient or more powerful tradition of the love of knowledge". In those days, the foundations of education lay in religion and religious activities. Life in all aspects was inspired by and infused with religion.

During the vedic period, 'Gurukula' method prevailed, in which the student lived in the house of the 'Guru' instead of living with his parents. Along with his colleagues, he led a systematic life and obtained education in the house of the Guru. The process of education passed through the three stages of comprehension, meditation, memory and nidhi-dhyasana. The Gurukulas were the centres of education, in which education was imparted only by individuals of character and ability. The student remained with his Guru for 12 years. Congresses of scholars were also organised from time to time. In these, awards were also given to prominent scholars.

The education in the Brahman age was, to a very great extent, only a refined and developed form of vedic education. In this age, art of writing had developed, and so both oral and written education came into practice, though the emphasis was upon oral education. Education was conducted through discussions, answering of questions, removal of doubts, etc. Practical work was emphasized in such subjects as grammar, astrology, nyaya, medicine, etc. The students as well as the teachers themselves obtained informal education from famous scholars.

During the Buddhist period, educational institutions for general education were established. They made provisions for imparting primary as well as higher education. An important contribution in this period was, the method of collective teaching and the presence of numerous in a single, institution was evolved. The system of determining a minimum age for higher education, providing a set of rules, and taking a test for admission are even today guiding the educational structure.

During the Muslim period, Muslim rulers took an interest in education. During this period, special stress was laid on the teaching of Arabic and Persian, and a new language called 'Urdu' was emerged from the inter-mixing of Arabic and Persian. It was profoundly influenced by Islam. Students were to memorise the 'Koran'. Importance was attached to a study of Islam. The spread of education only from the practical and materialistic view points. Education in manual skills, sculpture, agriculture, medicine, etc., is the proof of this knowledge. Military science, painting, housing construction, manufacture of weapons, etc., were also imparted. Knowledge of such subjects was given to students directly and individually by experts through a system of apprenticeship.

In earlier times, education was primarily meant for survival. Children were taught necessary skills for living. Gradually, however, man began to use education for a variety of purposes. Today, we realise that education may be used not only for purposes of survival, but also for a more enriched life, better use of leisure time and improvements in social and cultural life. Although the practice of education has developed along with the theories of education, many people often overlook this connection between theory and practice. We often seem to be more involved with the 'practical' aspects of education, and forget the theories behind it.

Education is the most powerful tool for change and hence it must train the minds of educated to cope with the change. Equally, the educational system throughout the length and breadth of India must actively promote that value system and outlook which is consistent with the kind of society we wish to establish. Finally, those who are thinking about education must realise that in the fast changing world of today no education system can be frozen into the mould.

Seen in this perspective, education is increasingly becoming a continuing process stretched over the entire life span of man in terms of the imagery 'from the lap to the grave'. It is available to the new generation as the quintessence of the accumulated social experience of mankind before its initiation into the world through leisure time activities, through the formal as well as non-formal channels, during the working age and it would steer the life of the aged in meaningful directions after retirement. Education of the future is bound to be united intimately with the life of mankind through every fibre of its being.

Importance of Education in Human Life

Children takes birth as a helpless creature, but his helplessness proves to be a blessing for him rather than a curse. Human child is not able to stand and walk at the time of his birth, he has to learn these activities. Where there is an ability to learn, there is a possibility of variety in learning. The childhood of man is much longer than that of other creatures. Animals and birds start behaving like adults within a short period of time whereas human child has to spend about twenty four years of his life learning how to behave like adults.

Learning is the nature of child. Child learns according to the demand of nature. From this point of view, it is the natural right of child to receive proper education. The famous educator Pestalozzi has said "Education is our birth right". He also said that education is a necessity and the society is responsible to make provision for it. The working of society is impossible without education or educated persons. The fulfilment of the needs of human life is possible only through education. By education man forms a proper attitude towards life. Education shows us some ways by which we can solve the problems of life. Life is full of struggles, and man makes his life successful by proper education and training. A Sanskrit poet has regarded education as a protector, a well wisher and an affectionate mother or a father or a wife.

Secondary Education

The need for improved levels of school participation and achievement is now globally accepted. The key role of schools in materialising this need is reflected in a variety of efforts to transform the nature and functions of education at various levels of school education in keeping with the cherished values and aspirations of the people for whom it is meant. In India, the constitutional commitment to the Universalisation of Elementary Education (U.E.E.) and Delhi Declaration in respect of Education for All (E.F.A.) are being hailed as very positive steps for ensuring the country's overall development. However, measures like the U.E.E. and E.F.A. are bound to have certain implications, the most immediate one being concerned with and related to the role of research and development in secondary education.

For one thing, secondary education is a link between elementary education and tertiary and higher education. It is evident that improved enrollment at the elementary stage has led to increased access to secondary schools which, in turn, has influenced demands for tertiary and higher education. Secondary education, thus, is of special importance in the educational ladder in as much as its successful completion is a requirement for admission into institutions of higher education and, at the same time, being a terminal stage, it caters to the needs of those who enter the world of work. Again, as stressed by the National Policy on Education, 1986, updated in 1992, "Secondary education exposes students to the differentiated roles of science, the humanities and social sciences. This is also an appropriate stage to provide children with a sense of history and national prospective and give them opportunities to understand their constitutional duties and rights as citizens".

Teaching

What is teaching? Ah! There you have the worst paid and the best rewarded of all vocations. By mercenary standards, teaching is poorly paid. It's riches are of another order, less tangible, but more lasting—the satisfaction of personal fulfilment. There is little reward in teaching for those who worship Mammon. There is much for those who worship God. Teaching is thus not everybody's cup of tea. It is not a soft option. It requires blood, sweat and tears. Teaching is considered to be an art. Children are the raw material with which the teacher has to deal. Addition points out that as "sculpture is to a block of marble, education is to the human soul". The teacher unconsciously designs the child entrusted to him. The teacher has a purpose and he modifies the child accordingly.

Teaching is a sublime art. It is impossible to separate the teacher and teaching. The teacher, in fact, mirrors himself into the child; he puts an indelible stamp on the young, growing plastic mind of the child. The child generally takes after the teacher.

Teaching today is very vaguely referred to as a profession in India. Surprisingly, no criteria have so far been evolved to evaluate its technical position. As seen, already, teaching in India is comparatively a 'new' vocation, especially a creation of the late 19th century, and is essentially patterned on its western counterpart. The reasons for adopting their criteria here would not only be rationally tenable but also logically correct. And the fact that in the west also, teaching as a secular vocation has passed through identical phases, the case for adopting their criteria gets still more strengthened. "The entry of the state into the establishment and support of schools gave powerful aid to the development of teaching as a profession".

The major author on the nature and organisation of professions, A.M. Carr-Saunders, says: "A little reflections shows that what we now call a profession emerges when a number of persons are found to be practicing a definite technique founded upon a specialized training. A profession may perhaps be defined as an occupation based upon specialised intellectual study and training, the purpose of which is to supply skilled, service and advice to others for a definite fee or salary."

Teaching is very much goal-oriented and a purposeful activity. It sets into motion a system of strategies for the realisation of certain definite and pre-determined objectives. These objectives may be formulated in accordance with the prevailing social philosophy, the intellectual level of students, the stage of education which teaching is done, and the demands which the students will have to meet in later life, or in the light of certain social and personal considerations. The concept of good or effective teaching is generally governed by its efficiency in achieving the desired results.

From the point of view of students, good teaching is that which takes care of their own objectives in acquiring knowledge. This analysis of knowledge in time perspective has important implications according to the point of view of teaching. Knowledge as an objective of teaching, thus, gets a continuous time frame, the past, the present and the future. It helps in relating research with teaching, and enriching teaching with constant inflow of new knowledge into the content to be taught.

Teaching of facts and do's and don'ts of today may be of transitory importance, but what is of greater importance is to build a perspective, a point of view from which to examine knowledge and facts. Teaching may, therefore, deal with information on knowledge and facts, but should soon lead on to higher mental functions and capacities.

Teacher

Our ancestors gave the third place to the teacher in society; the first being the Mother, the second Father and the fourth place to the God. The influence of the first two persons are inevitable for each and every child in their home atmosphere and then only the children proceed to the next sacred place of learning, i.e., school, and where they are being affected by the various situations of classrooms. So, that is why, it is said that "The parent is the first teacher of a child and the teacher is the second parent of the child". Now-a-days, each pupil is being taught by a number of teachers who differ in their way of teaching and in the same way the pupils also vary in their achievements, either in one subject or in different subjects taught by different teachers in the classrooms.

Teacher is given the highest place in the society. He is regarded as a person to lead the humanity on proper lines. Teacher's place is next to parents. Our Sanskrit sloka says this fact that "Mathrudevobhava, Pitrudevobhava, Acharyadevobhava". Another sloka compares Guru with God that "Guru Brahma, Guru Vishnu, Gurudevo Maheswarah, Guru Sakshat Para Brahma Tasmai Sri Gurave Namaha". Guru is compared with Trimurthies, the creator, the protector and the destroyer of the world. Ultimately the teacher is considered as God himself. The teacher has secured supreme respect and regard as he aims at building of character, social efficiency and spreading of national culture.

Each teacher has been termed the "Torch-bearer" of the race, the one who by the light of his knowledge, removes the darkness of ignorance. He moulds the lives of thousands of children and is known as the builder of the nation. He dedicates of his life to the service of others and symbolises a candle which burns to light the way for others. In the words of *Ross*, "The teacher, in a naturalistic set-up, is only a setter of the stage; a supplier of material and opportunities; a provider of an ideal environment; a creator of conditions under which natural development takes place".

In the words of Tagore, "A teacher can never truly teach unless he is still learning himself. A lamp can never light another lamp unless it continues to burn its own flame. A teacher who has come to the end of his subject, who has no living traffic with his knowledge but merely repeats his lessons to the students, he cannot question them. The greater part of our learning in the schools has been waste, because for most of our teachers and their students are like dead specimens of once living things, with which they have a learned acquaintance but no communication of life and love".

A teacher is one who imparts knowledge to the pupils. When a teacher is doing or helping some one else to learn, he or she is teaching. It is also important to keep in mind that the quality of teaching is directly related to the quality and the value of learning that is taking place in his students. Further, there is no best way to teach what a teacher should do at a particular moment is not something that can be determined from any scientific formula. Successful teachers, like other artists, develop their own ways of getting the results they seek.

In a way, all the teachers those who are in teaching profession from kindergarten to University level may not be teaching or behaving uniformly well to the extent of the satisfaction of their students, at least in the classroom situations. We expect that a teacher should be a good model or a leader; so as to be imitated by his/her students both within and outside the classroom situations. The inter-relationship between the teachers and the taught was well expressed with a degree of difference among teachers through a good saying that:

"The mediocre teacher tells,

The good teacher explains,

The superior teacher demonstrates, and

The great teacher inspires".

Among these teachers, the last category would highly be limited and perhaps majority of them would come in the first category and the rest of the teachers may come under the remaining two categories.

Schools are the nurseries of the nation and the teachers and the architects of the future society. So the role of the teachers is crucial in the teaching learning process. Though the worlds like Teacher-Effectiveness, Teacher-Competence or Teaching-Success are used synonymously, they are different. Rajagopalan. S. (1976) described Teacher Effectiveness as an ability to produce good results. Whatever it may be, the teacher must have certain qualities like.

(i) Mastering of the Subject Matter.

(ii) Proper Professional Training.

(iii) Love of the Profession.

(iv) Love for Children and Knowledge of Psychology.

(v) Honesty, Politeness, Sincerity, Patience and Tolerance.

(vi) Sense of Humour, Patriotism and Sympathy.

(vii) Being Friend, Philosopher and Guide.

(viii) Sound Physical and Mental Health.

(ix) Preparation for Classroom Teaching and so on.

The present-day teacher in India is a by-product of the emergence of the middle class in the latter half of the 19th century. In spite of some of the ruminants of the glory of the past that are attached to his calling to this day, it is difficult to maintain that he is a direct linear descendant of his illustrious fore father. Indeed, but for the striking similarities between the jobs, the two–the past and present teachers—have performed, or continue to perform, the differences and the distinctions in their social and economic position are so pronouncedly marked that one could ignore them only at the risk of perpetuating a myth, a legend which is as misleading as it is false. If the aura of his high social status has continued in the lay mind, it is more because a lack of any precise, objective clarification of his role rather than due to any public performance for him.

The outstanding features of the teacher during the ancient and medieval period should, therefore, constitute; his priestly character, restricted purpose, and an uneventful life in a more or less stable society. The fact that he was more a priest than a teacher, as we understand by the term, contributed singularly to his high social esteem. When the British period appeared in the early 17th century, the Indian teacher, both Hindu and Muslim, was working on the social periphery—in far away places without the sense of cohesion and practical purpose.

These days when so many sudden and sweeping changes are occurring both in the content areas and methodologies of teaching, we all know how knowledge in all areas gets outdated soon. The pace of research in all content areas is very fast. Consequently, a good teacher must find time to remain reasonably up-to-date and this must have its reflections on his earnings and also social life. So a teacher today will have to take care of his equipment himself.

The modern teacher has to take into account the new mores that are already around him to unravel, interpret and implement. He has not merely to shed the old attitudes and value patterns but replace them with new, more constructive and meaningful concepts and values. The teacher has to have faith in himself, in the future of the nation and the socialist philosophy of life and relationships.

The good teacher has to be up-to-date and future-oriented. He is charged with the responsibility of building up the nation through better teaching, good human relationships and problem solving attitude formation. Incidentally, this problem-solving approach is a very important change and the ever-increasing complexities enjoin upon the teacher to learn how to resolve problems.

Statement of the Problem

A study of the Problems of Private Secondary School Teachers

Need of the Study

Now-a-days, teaching profession is the most valuable and more important of all the professions. Teachers are the future builders of the nation. It is the most devotable and noblest profession. To give justice to the profession, teachers shouldn't have any burdens or problems. Then only they can concentrate on teaching.

Problems of teachers are never heard of in the ancient past, particularly in India. Today, teacher suffers from innumerable problems and in spite of his variant efforts, is yet to come out of these. The teachers are made the scapegoats and the society is coming out ruthlessly criticising the teachers. It is true that there is a change in the role played by the past teacher from the present teacher. However, a careful examination of the present day teacher reveals that he plays comparatively a minor role in the present decorative educational standards of the country. The position of the present day teacher, especially the private school teacher, is so insignificant that he can hardly be responsible for any draw-backs in the field of education.

So the researchers took the problems faced by the private school teachers for study.

Objectives of the Study

The objectives of the present study are:

1. To find out the problems of the private secondary school teachers.
2. To find out the problems of men and women teachers working in private secondary schools.
3. To find out the problems of teachers working in recognised and unrecognised private secondary schools.
4. To find out the problems of science and social studies teachers working in private secondary schools.

Scope of the Study

The present investigation aims to identify the problems of private secondary school teachers of Vijayawada. This study is limited to the teachers working in private secondary schools functioning in Vijayawada corporation only. Variables such as sex, recognition of the school, and teaching subjects of the teachers are considered.

2

Related Literature

The survey of related studies implies locating, studying and evaluating reports of relevant researches, study of published articles, going through related portions of Encyclopaedias and research abstracts, study of pertinent pages out of comprehensive books on the subject and going through related manuscripts if any. For any worthwhile study in any field of knowledge, the research worker needs an adequate familiarity with the work which has already been done in the area of his choice. He needs to acquire up-to-date information about what has been thought and done in the particular area. He has to build upon the accumulated and recorded knowledge of the past to draw maximum benefit from the designs and procedures of previous researches, to match his conclusions with the conclusions drawn earlier and to add from his side a line or two to the existing store of knowledge.

Research takes the advantage of the knowledge which has accumulated in the past as a result of constant human endeavour. It can never be undertaken in isolation of the work that has already been done on the problems which are directly or indirectly related to a study proposed by a researcher. A review of the related literature must precede any well planned research study.

The review of the literature is an important part of the scientific approach and is carried out in all areas of scientific research, whether in the physical, natural or social sciences. Such reviews are also the basis of most research in the humanities. The review of the literature in educational research provides with the means of getting to the frontier in a particular field of knowledge. Until the researcher has learned what others have done and what remains still to be done in his area, he cannot develop a research project that will contribute to furthering knowledge in his field. Thus, the literature in any field forms the foundation upon which all future work must be built. The researcher is always tempted to let a sketchy review of the literature suffice, so that he can get started sooner on his own research project. The researcher, however, should make every effort to complete a thorough review before starting his research because the insights and knowledge gained by the review almost inevitably lead to a better designed project and greatly improve the chances of obtaining important and significant results. Often the insights gained through the review will save the researcher as much time in conducting his project as the review itself required.

Although the general purpose of the review is to help the researcher develop a thorough understanding and insight into previous work and the trends that have emerged, the review can also help in reaching a number of important specific goals.

Secondary Education

There is a special emphasis on processes in secondary education, including need-based course in both the liberal arts and the vocational streams; curriculum planning, including the methodology of teaching and evaluation procedures and educational technology; new approaches in teacher preparation; better health and nutrition; national unity; and international understanding and co-operation. Schemes are being developed to provide access to secondary education facilities to the maximum number of people, and especially to those belonging to the backward areas.

The term secondary education is imprecise and there is considerable divergence in the national definitions of secondary education. In some places, secondary education begins at 11, in others at 12. The Education Commission (1964-66) suggests the term 'primary education' for the first seven to eight years and the term 'secondary education' for the following four to five pre-university years. The five years of secondary education are divided into two cycles—lower secondary corresponding to 14, 15 and 16 (classes VIII, IX and X) and higher secondary corresponding to 17 and 18 (classes XI and XII). It is clear that such usage of the terms of a specific age-range is essentially administrative.

Psychologically, secondary education has often been defined as education of the adolescent. But research findings have clearly established that the growth of a child cannot be divided into clear-cut stages. The popular belief that 11 or 12 is a psychological water-shed which is no longer tenable. Different people cross from childhood into adolescence and from adolescence into adult life at different ages. Also, a person may linger behind childhood in some aspects of life, long after becoming adult in other ways. Physiological and psychological growth can no longer be assumed to proceed at precisely the same pace and social pressures may easily push boys and girls into social maturity earlier than personal maturity.

Consequently, the view that the process of education is a continuous one in which changes in curriculum and methods should occur gradually according to the needs and levels of development of children is gaining ground in most places. In many countries, the entire school period is now treated as a unified whole and the terms 'primary' and 'secondary' appear to have lost all value even administratively and are now tending to drop out of use. Examples of countries where the problems of articulation between primary and secondary education appear to have been successfully overcome by treating the entire school stage as a unified system are Denmark, Sweden, East European States and erstwhile Soviet Union.

During the British period, secondary education in India was considered by a number of important commissions or study groups on different occasions. The basic objectives of secondary education were invariably stated in terms such as liberal education, training of the mind, development of personality, preparation for the responsibilities of adult life, etc., and the main concern throughout this period was with standards, the need to rescue secondary education from the domination of the matriculation examination and its diversification, so that for a great majority of pupils it could serve as a terminal stage.

The first serious attempt to look, among other things, into the objectives of secondary education after independence was made by the Secondary Education Commission (Mudaliar Commission, 1952-53). The Commission stated three broad objectives:

(i) preparation for the responsibilities of democratic citizenship;

(ii) improvement of productive efficiency enabling the national wealth to increase and the standard of living of the people to be raised appreciably; and

(iii) development of the cultural and aesthetic aspects of the child's personality.

Elaborating the concept of democratic citizenship, the Commission stated that "The objective of a democratic education is, therefore, the full all round development of every individual's personality. This requires that education should take into account of all his needs—psychological, social, emotional and practical and cater to all of them".

For improving productive efficiency of secondary school leavers, the Commission recommended, inter-alia, diversification of courses, so that a large number of students could take up agricultural, technical, commercial or other practical courses which would train their varied aptitudes and enable them either to take up vocational pursuits at the end of the secondary course or to join technical institutions for further training.

The underlying idea of cultural or aesthetic development, according to the Commission was that "the pupils go out with more sensitive and quickened minds that can respond readily to the numerous stimuli in the world of Art and Nature".

The objectives of secondary education as stated by the Mudaliar Commission are very similar to the objectives of secondary education in many other parts of the world. As examples: According to the Spens Report on Secondary Education (1938) "a school fulfils its proper purposes in so far as it fosters that growth, helping every boy and girl to achieve the highest degree of individual development of which he or she is capable". The Norwood Report (1941) explained the main aim of education is to provide "the nature and the environment which will enable the child to grow a right and to grow eventually to full stature; to bring to full flowering the varying potentialities, physical, spiritual and intellectual, of which he is capable as an individual and as a member of society". According to the Newsom Committee (1963), the general objectives of education are the cultivation of basic skills, qualities of character, knowledge and physical well-being. Further, the value of experience of education "should be assessed in terms of its total impact on the pupil's skills, qualities and personal development, not by basic attainments alone".

It is clear that while statements of educational objectives serve to emphasize one or two special points particularly relevant to the stage in question, they reveal a broad underlying identity of purposes. At the primary stage of education, for instance, one comes across a specific mention of the three Rs, that is, development of communication skills in reading and writing and mastery of number operations. If no mention of these is made at the subsequent stages, it is because at this stages, these are simply taken for granted. Similarly, at the secondary stage, one often comes across a special mention of the need to attend to the interests and aptitudes of pupils. This is not because interests and aptitudes in many cases seen for the first time to emerge with reasonable clarity.

Nature of Teaching

In order to understand the nature of teaching, it is necessary to know what teaching is not. Teaching is not merely imparting knowledge to students, nor is it merely giving advice. Some people think that teaching is passing to the class one's own experience. Some define that "Teaching is hearing the students recite their lessons" or "Teaching is hearing the students memorise what they read in the textbook". All these definitions give a narrow view of teaching.

Ryburn has widened the scope of teaching by giving it another function. He says that "It should include the training of the emotions of the child. Teaching is one of the means of giving right feelings to children". Mursell in his famous book "Successful Teaching" says that "teaching is not so much the direction or the guidance of learning as the organisation of learning". Mursell prefers the words "organisation of learning", because it includes guidance and direction of learning experiences and something more than else.

To sum up, "Teaching is establishing a harmonious relationship between teacher, pupil and subject, it is giving useful information, it is causing the child to learn, it is the stimulation and direction of learning, it is helping the child to make effective adjustments, it is guiding the pupil activity, and it is training of his emotions".

Role of the Teacher

The Report of Commonwealth Conference (1974) has stated the role of the teacher as: "The teacher has a major role in educational development whether he approaches his work actively or passively. He can influence development adversely by opposing innovation or merely remaining mute in the face of a growing need for reform; on the other hand, he can participate actively as an initiator himself or an interpreter of the plans devised by others".

The Education Commission (1964-66) has emphasised the role of the teacher in the following words: "Of all different factors which influence the quality of education and its contribution to national development, the quality competence and character of teachers are undoubtedly the most significant. Nothing is more important than securing a sufficient supply of high quality recruits to the teaching profession, providing them with the best possible professional preparation and creating satisfactory conditions of work in which they can be fully effective".

It has rightly been said in the Report of Commonwealth Conference (1974) that in order to be competent: "The teacher must have the knowledge of child development, of the material to be taught and suitable methods of teaching it, of the culture of his pupils (which may not be his own) and of some interest of his own; his skills must enable him to teach, advise and guide his pupils, community and culture with which he is involved; his attitudes should be positive without being aggressive, so that his example is likely to be followed as he transmits explicity and implicity the national aims and ideals and moral and social values".

In the past half century, therefore, most studies have focused on teacher behaviours and teaching practices in an attempt to define good teacher can be inferred from the results of these studies. Good teachers clearly delineate goals or intended outcomes; they select or develop a curriculum that is linked directly with these goals or intended outcomes; and they are able to "deliver" the defined curriculum to the students. Despite this composite definition, many teachers are not successful in one or more of these three key elements. First, some teachers have no explicit goals or fail to make their goals explicit to their students. Second, for some teachers, the curriculum is misaligned with the tests used to judge the success of both student learning and classroom teaching. Third, standardized approaches to instructional delivery are being advocated by many educators at the same time that researchers are suggesting the context bound nature of effective teaching.

Presently, a certain consistency emerges from a careful consideration of existing research studies concerning the qualities and practices of effective teachers, such teachers are more concerned with "ends" than with "means". They care more about the impact of their behaviour on students than on how that behaviour might look to an outside observer. They thrive on accomplishment of their students and, ultimately, their own as teachers. Because of this, these teachers develop a "sense of efficacy".

At the same time, effective teachers possess those characteristics that we have valued in teachers for generations: they know their subject well enough to teach it; they care about their student and treat them with respect; they are able to make wise and prudent decisions. Although, some people are naturally predisposed toward these practices, the knowledge that has been gained through research enables us to develop strategies and techniques that permit the production of large number of more effective teachers.

Teacher effectiveness will be used to refer to the results a teacher gets or to the amount of the progress the pupils make toward some specified goal of education. One implication of this definition is that teacher effectiveness must be defined, and can only be assessed, in terms of behaviours of teachers (Medley, 1982). Teacher effectiveness can be contrasted with teacher performance and teacher competence. Teacher performance refers to the behaviour of a teacher while teaching a class (Medley, 1982). Obviously, not all beahviours produce results. Finally, teacher competence is "the set of knowledges, abilities and beliefs a teacher possesses and brings to the teaching situation...The knowledge, skills and beliefs in a teacher's repertoire will be referred to as 'competencies' that the teacher possesses" (Medly, 1982). An effective teacher is able to use the existing competencies to achieve the desired results.

Job Satisfaction and Teachers' Problems

Uniyal (1976) found that the teachers of private schools displayed higher level of anxiety than government school teachers regarding their job satisfaction. He also hypothesised that the teachers in government schools enjoy more freedom than the teachers working under private managements.

Anjaneyulu (1968) found that the factors which contributed to dissatisfaction were lack of academic freedom and heavy work-load.

Gangappa (1969) stated that the multiplicity of tasks and duties makes one loose his job, and subjects him to all kinds of worries and maladjustments.

Ahmad (1984) found that the most important predictors for teachers feeling of job satisfaction were the amount of pay offered by the job, the degree of help received from superiors, and the amount of say teachers had in decision making. Least important predictors for job satisfaction were found to be opportunity for promotion and the degree of fairness of work load.

Economic Status and Teachers' Problems

The teacher's economic status was the crux of all problems; the pay scales were hardly sufficient to meet the present cost of living in a fair and just manner.

Srivastava, V. (1979) in his study "A study of sense of responsibility among secondary school teachers" found that the teachers belonging to families having income of more than Rs. 1000 per month scored significantly higher on the sense of responsibility scale than the teachers belonging to families having an income of less than Rs. 1000 per month.

Tali, R. (1984) in his study "A study of problems faced by high school teachers and their attitude towards teaching profession in Nalgonda" found that low pay scale, absence of professional status, lack of recognition by society, and appointment of unqualified teachers were some important reasons for low status of teachers.

Trivedi, K.P. (1961) in his study "The social and economic conditions of Rural Secondary Teachers in Uttar Pradesh" found that the personal aspects of the rural teachers' life was marked by large joint families, unsatisfactory living conditions and deprivation of many civic, social and cultural amenities of life.

Rawoot (1959) in his study "The problems of teachers working in primary and secondary schools" found that the prevailing discontentment of teachers working in primary schools of Dharwar district was with their socio-economic status and the discontentment of parents with the inefficiency of teachers.

Philips (1961) studied some problems of adjustment in the early years of a teacher's life. The problems mentioned by the investigator were personality difficulties, social or economic problems and professional problems.

Age and Teachers' Problems

Singh, U.P. (1987) in his study "A study of the extent and the patterns of reactions to frustration and professional adjustment of secondary school teachers" found that the teachers of the upper-age group were found to be more frustrated than the teachers of the lower age group. The teachers of the upper age-group were found to be more fluctuating in nature in compassion with teachers of the lower age-group. There was no effect of sex, status, residence, experience and academic stream on fixation of teachers.

Srivastava, U. (1979) in his study "A study of sense of responsibility among secondary school teachers" found that the younger teachers in the age range of twenty to thirty yeas scored the highest and the older teachers in the age range of fifty to sixty scored the lowest on the sense of responsibility scale. The sense of responsibility in the teaching profession decreased as age increased.

Sex and Teachers' Problems

Passi and Sharma (1982) in their study entitled "A study of teaching competency of secondary school teachers" found that the male teachers scored significantly higher on the characteristic of dutifulness than the female teachers. There was no significant difference between the male and female teachers with respect to disciplinarianism. The female teachers showed a higher degree of firm determination than their male counterparts.

Singh, V.P. (1987) in his study "A study of the extent and the patterns of reactions to frustration and professional adjustment of secondary school teachers" found that the male teachers were more aggressive than female teachers.

Shanti Kumar (1961) in his study "The problems confronted by women teachers" found that 91 per cent of women teachers took up the teaching profession because they were inclined towards teaching but they had problems of adjustment in their personal and social life.

Experience and Teachers' Problems

Singh, V.P. (1987) in his study found that teachers having less teaching experience showed a greater rationalising tendency than teachers with more experience.

Srivastava, U. (1979) in his study "A study of sense of responsibility among secondary school teachers" found that the graduate teachers of less experience showed significantly more sense of responsibility than the post-graduate and more experienced teachers.

Language and Non-language Teachers' Problems

Passi, B.K. and Sharma (1982) in their study "A study of teaching competency of secondary school teachers" found that there was positive significant correlation between the age of the language teachers teaching at secondary level and their teaching competency. There was no significant relationship of the attitude of the language teachers teaching English/Hindi at the secondary level towards teaching, interest, intelligence with teaching competency. There was a significant negative correlation between the self-perception of the language teachers teaching at secondary level and teaching competency.

Madhu, V. (1978) in his study "A study of the problems of secondary school teachers of Nalgonda district in teaching Biological Science" found that most of the teachers were teaching other subjects besides biological sciences. A majority of teachers had studied other subjects besides biological sciences. Film strips, insect cages, microscopes and physiological apparatus were not adequately available for biology teaching.

Syama Sundara Rao (1971) in his study "The problems faced by the teachers in the teaching of social studies in the secondary schools" found that adequate facilities to try out new methods are not provided in schools, the schools do not have adequate reference material, and adequate programmes for the improvement of professional competence are lacking.

Management and Teachers' Problems

Trivedi, K.P. (1961) in his study "The social and economic conditions of rural secondary teachers in Uttar Pradesh" found that malpractices of the management in the aided and especially in the unaided institutions undermined the teachers confidence and capacities as well as the human and social significance of his profession.

Anjaneyulu (1968) in his study "The job satisfaction of teachers in secondary schools of Andhra Pradesh" observed that teachers working in private schools were dissatisfied because of lack of security, rigid and orthodox service conditions and too much domination by the management.

California Institute of Technology (1953-54) conducted a series of surveys of employee opinion and concluded that the employees expressed a great desire for information from management.

Sommers (1969) observed that most of the teachers felt that there was a lack of communication between teachers and administrators.

Bernard and Kulandaivel (1976) in their study "Job satisfaction of high school teachers working under different managements" found that the teachers of government aided private schools appeared to be better satisfied than the teachers from municipal and government schools. It was also found that teachers working under different managements had different problems.

Efficiency and Teachers' Problems

Tali, R. (1984) in his study "A study of problems faced by high school teachers and their attitude towards teaching profession in Nalgonda" found that teachers worked under heavy pressure of problems pertaining to various aspects of the teaching profession. The problems faced particularly in the areas of academic work, job conditions, financial status and within and outside school interaction appeared to be common, which appear to have adversely affected the quality of teaching and efficiency of teachers. Knowledge of psychology, interest in teaching subject, better mastery of the subject, and proper assessment of work were perceived as effective measures for improving teachers' performance.

Trivedi, K.P. (1961) in his study "The social and economic conditions of rural secondary school teachers in Uttar Pradesh" found that the reasons for the lack of quality personnel were the unsatisfactory service conditions and lack of a flexible, efficient and organised programme of recruitment because of the unattractive pay, insecurity of job, uncertainty of prospects, irregularity in payment and insufficient provision for leisure.

Jewett (1958) after many long years of study found that teachers were disillusioned by conditions which prevented their performance at quality level. Clerical routines, teaching load, pupil teacher relations and community projects were among the chief reasons for this complaining.

Facilities and Teachers' Problems

Madhu, V. (1978) in his study "A study of the problems of secondary school teachers of Nalgonda district in teaching Biological Sciences" found that a majority of the teachers stated that they did not have adequate classroom facilities. Ninety three per cent of teachers stated that they did not have separate periods for practicals in Biology. Most of the teachers were over-burdened with work-load. In most of the schools, teachers were experiencing inadequate laboratory facilities.

Tali, R. (1984) in his study "A study of problems faced by high school teachers and their attitude towards teaching profession in Nalgonda" found that a high percentage of teachers perceived better service conditions, better academic programmes and facilities, adequate housing and other facilities, lighter work load as professional needs.

David (1978) made an investigation into "The economic, academic, administrative and social needs of rural primary teachers" and found that most of the primary school teachers were worried much about inadequate facilities and misuse of administrative powers by both officials and non-officials.

Syama Sundara Rao (1971) in his study "The problems faced by the teachers in the teaching of social studies in the secondary schools" found that the schools do not have adequate reference material, work load of teachers is heavy, and the teachers received step-motherly treatment from their managements.

The Research Division of the National Educational Association, U.S.A. (1967) summarised research studies on teacher load and pointed out that continued efforts for smaller classes, more time for planning and freedom from unnecessary tensions and relief from duties would contribute to the teachers satisfaction.

G.L. Nagapal (1972) in his study "The nature of problems faced by the teachers working in secondary schools in the border areas of Punjab" found that only one-third of the total number of teachers were punctual in attending the schools. The reason was that the teachers had to live at distances ranging around 30 kms away from the place of work. The lack of such basic necessities of the life like means of transport, good family life, of entertainment, etc., effected the working of these teachers.

Marital Status and Teachers' Problems

Srivastava, U. (1979) found that the unmarried teachers scored' significantly higher on the sense of responsibility scale than the married teachers.

3

Design of the Research

A research design is a plan of action, a plan for collecting data in an economic, efficient and relevant manner. So the design of the study is the heart of any research. The following aspects have been discussed in detail which are related with the design of the present study entitled "A study of the problems of private secondary school teachers". The research procedure includes explaining operational definitions of different terms used in the study, the various hypotheses framed for verification in the present study and the rational of these hypotheses. The selection of sample includes the sampling techniques used, the reasons for selection of a particular sampling technique and the selection of the sample according to different variables. The selection of the tools includes the selection of suitable tool for collection of data, description of the tool selected, testing its suitability for the present study and the procedure followed in administrating the tool to collect data.

Operational Definitions of Key Terms

The following terms have their importance in this study.

Private Schools

The schools managed by private organisations or individuals, either partially or totally, were known as private schools. The public schools, government recognised and aided schools were also included in private schools.

In Andhra Pradesh, some schools are run by State Government and some schools are run by Central Government to educate the children. The schools managed by Zilla Praja Parishads, Mandal or Panchayath Samithis and Municipal Councils are known as Government Schools. It is not possible to run adequate number of schools by the government itself. So, to fulfil the needs of the society, some private organisations, religious bodies, trust boards and some individuals started secondary schools. These schools are called the private schools.

The Teacher

Education is the only instrument which alone can bring a drastic change in the society. India need education by right teachers. It is a universally accepted fact that teachers has a significant, meaningful, obligatory and morally responsible role in education, ideolistic or realistic. If education is regarded as an instrument, then the teachers are the men, who will move and handle this instrument to activity. As an instrument, education cannot function itself. So it requires the help of the teachers to become active and operative.

The teachers should posses comprehensive knowledge and wisdom. A teacher should feel that it is his duty to show a right way through their teaching. Teachers should first observe and identify the needs of the student and they should show compassion on them and respond to their needs with their teaching. There are some teachers with a vast knowledge in different subjects, yet they are unable to teach the students efficiently. Some teachers have a little knowledge in a particular field or subject, still they can impress the students with their knowledge. So, it is not the matter of how highly qualified a teacher is, but how best he can impress the students.

A real teacher is one who sacrifices his life for his students. He teaches them as he teaches his own children. Besides imparting knowledge to the students, he makes them aware of virtues like love, compassion, self-control, unselfishness, truth and purity in thought, word and deed. It is the teacher who plays an important role in moulding and shaping the personality of a student. Such a teacher can be described as a "Maker of new age". He can love and inspire the students and therefore make his profession noble. A teacher is one who teaches in a school.

Secondary School Teachers

Those who are working in secondary schools are called secondary school teachers.

Secondary School Teachers' Problems

Secondary school teachers' problems are many and various. These could be professional and academic in nature; personal and interpersonal; and problems related to administration, management and the general motivation and over all job satisfaction of the teachers. When compared, teachers working in different schools are facing different types of problems. So, the present study investigates the problems of teachers working in private secondary schools.

Variables of the Study

Variables are the conditions or characteristics that the experimenter manipulates, controls or observes.

The variables considered for the present study were:

1. Men and women teachers working private secondary schools.
2. Teachers working in private recognised and unrecognised secondary schools.
3. Science and social studies teachers working in private secondary schools.

The rationale for choosing the above variables is discussed here with.

Men and Women Teachers

Many researchers in the past identified a difference in the performance and problems of men and women teachers. In the present study, both sexes were included to find out whether there is any significant difference between the problems of men and women teachers.

Recognised and Unrecognised School Teachers

Private school teachers including both recognised and unrecognised schools are recruited by the school correspondents or the board of management of the schools. They do not get such facilities like retirement benefits, promotion to higher posts compared to teachers working in government schools. The work and conduct of the teachers in these schools will be closely observed by the management. There is no question of transfer of teachers. But, the government involvement is there in recognised schools. So, there may be a difference in the problems faced by the recognised and unrecognised secondary school teachers.

Science and Social Studies Teachers

The education, orientation, system, work, etc., are different in teaching science and social studies. Because of this reason, in the present study, science and social studies teachers were taken as variables to identify the problems which are different from each other.

Hypotheses of the Study

The hypothesis is the most important step in the research process. It is a tentative supposition or provisional guess which seems to explain the situation under observation. The following hypotheses were formulated based on the variables and objectives of the study. These were stated in "Null hypothesis" form. The null hypothesis states that there is no significant difference or relationship between two or more parameters. It concerns to a judgement as to whether apparent differences or relationships are true differences or relationships or whether they merely result from sampling error.

Hypothesis 1

There are no problems to the private secondary schools teachers.

Hypothesis 2

There is no significant difference between the problems of men and women teachers working in private secondary schools.

Hypothesis 3

There is no significant difference between the problems of teachers working in recognised and unrecognised private secondary schools.

Hypothesis 4

There is no significant difference between the problems of science and social studies teachers working in private secondary schools.

Sample of the Study

After finalising the variables of the present study, consideration was given to whether the entire population is to be made the subject for data collection or a particular group is to be selected as representative of the whole population. The 'entire population' here refers to all the science and social studies teachers working in private secondary schools of Vijayawada.

Of the above two techniques, the selection of a group as a representative of whole population was found to be more suitable and convenient. The number of teachers selected will be small, and so it is possible to make a detailed and intensive study. This leads to more accurate and reliable results. So, this sampling technique was selected by the researcher for the collection of data.

In any social research, various methods are used for selection and drawing of samples. After a detailed study of all these methods, the stratified sampling method was found to be the most suitable method for the present research work.

At times, it is advisable to subdivide the population into smaller homogenous groups to get more accurate representation. This method results in the stratified random sample. Stratified random sampling is a refinement of simple random sampling since, in addition to randomness, stratification introduces a secondary element of control as a means of increasing precision and representativeness.

A stratified random sample is, in effect, a weighted combination of random sub-samples joined to give an over-all sample value. Since a random sample, may, by chance have an undue proportion of one type of unit in it, it is advisable to use stratified random sampling.

In the stratified sampling method, the entire population will be divided into smaller homogenous groups or strata, and then a sample is selected within each group. Every sampling unit in the population is placed is one of the strata prior to the selection of the sample so that the sum of the strata is identified with the population.

When employing the method of stratified random sampling, the researcher divides his population into different strata by some characteristic which is known from previous research or theories to be related to the phenomenon under investigation, and from each of the smaller homogeneous groups falling in each strata he draws randomly a predetermined number of units. Thus, in addition to randomness, stratification introduces a secondary element of control as a means of increasing precision and representativeness.

Stratified random sample is very much useful when lists of units or individuals in the population are not available. This method has been found practical even for small finite populations when cent per cent response is difficult to secure in the desired time. Stratified random sample provides more accurate results than simple random sampling only if stratification results in greater homogeneity within the strata, with respect to trait under study than it would be found in the whole population taken as a unit.

In order to develop a clear understanding of the theory and process of sampling, it is essential to know some important related terms.

In the technical phraseology of research, the whole population out of which the samples are selected is known as the universe. It means all those people who are proposed to be covered under the scheme of study. For the present research work, the universe includes all the science and social studies teachers working in private secondary schools of Andhra Pradesh. The study was limited to a particular geographical area, viz., Vijayawada, to facilitate appropriate sample selection and to avoid wastage of time and money.

A sample is a small proportion of a population selected for observation and analysis. By observing the characteristics of the sample, one can make certain inferences about the characteristics of the population from which it is drawn. Contrary to some popular opinion, samples are not selected haphazardly; they are chosen in a systematically random way, so that chance or the operation of probability can be utilized.

Besides considering these factors, it is most important to think about the size of the sample to be selected. If the sample is either too large or too small, it will make the study difficult and the results untenable. The size of sample for the present study was decided after considering the following factors:

1. A very large number of samples was not selected while a critical study was planned. A smaller sample will be convenient when compared with large number of sample.
2. The size and selection of the samples are also influenced by the nature of the universe. If the universe is homogeneous, even a small-sized sample may yield dependable and required results. If the universe is heterogeneous, small-sized samples may not be useful. In case of the present study, heterogeneous universe was split into smaller homogeneous groups, and samples were selected from these strata. For example, the private secondary school teachers of Vijayawada were broadly grouped under social studies and science teachers. A sample was selected from each of these two groups.
3. The researcher needs to determine the number of groups to be formed. In case the number of groups proposed is large, the size of the samples shall have to be large, and the large samples cannot fulfil the

requirement. In case the number of groups proposed is small, the small-sized samples can fulfil the requirement. In case of the present study, the universe is divided into male and female teachers, private recognised and unrecognised school teachers, science and social studies teachers. Since the number of groups was moderate, a reasonable sample was selected from each of these groups.

4. The size of sample is also influenced by the size of the tools to be used. If the tools are short, then a large sample can be selected or if the tools are large, then a small sample can be selected, so that from administrative point of view, the researcher may not be put to any unnecessary troubles. In the present study, as the tool is concerned with the problems of the teachers, a very large sample was not selected.

5. The sampling method also determines the size of the sample. When random sampling method is used, the samples have to be large. On the other hand, if samples are selected through stratified sampling method, the reliability can be achieved even with the help of the small-sized samples.

Taking these factors into consideration, it was decided that an ideal sample would consist of 80 private secondary school teachers. This sample is small enough to avoid unnecessary expenditure and large enough to avoid intolerable sampling errors.

Tool of the Study

A research tool plays a major role in any worthwhile research as it is the sole factor in determining the sound data and in arriving at perfect conclusions about the problem or study on hand, which ultimately, helps in providing suitable remedial measures to the problem concerned.

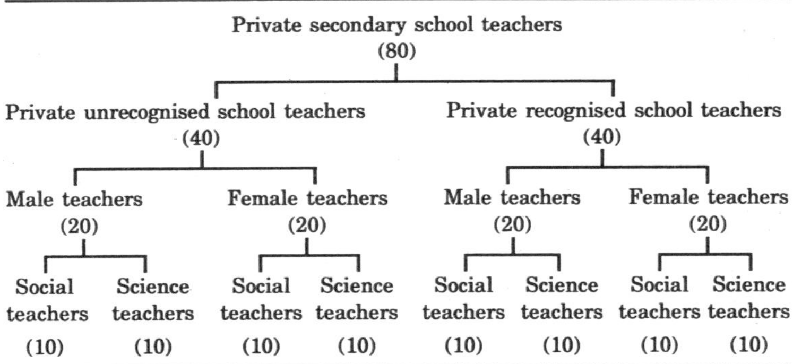

The selection and use of tools can be done in two ways. The first one is to construct a tool independently by the researcher for his own study. Here, there are many problems in doing so. On construction of own tools, Anand and Padma felt that 'A note of caution has to be struck when a researcher develops a tool for his study by merely pooling up some statements and does not subject it to the sophisticated techniques of tool construction'. The result would be then, obviously, a poor quality research. With this, one can say that preparation and standardization of tools is a major task, and one should take care in aspects like selection of area and sample, pooling up of statements related to the area, consulting the experts, and application of sophisticated statistical techniques.

The other way of selection and use of tools is right selection of tools from already standardized ones available in the field of study. Here also, it involves a tedious job in locating tools and identifying their usefulness to the study on hand. Even then, this technique is very useful when a research work is taken to study in depth and when the research work involves a good number of variables. Some people believe that some of the instruments available do not measure upto their standards. Hence, new ones. In some instances, consideration should be given to the logistics of the situation. Lacking time and financial resources for the construction of a test, many researchers can not expect to produce a better instrument. In these cases, the most logical procedure that one can follow is to choose the best instrument available for his purpose.

Considering the merits and limitations of the selection or preparation of tools, the researchers have no option other than constructing a tool for the present study as there are no standardized tools on the subject.

The researcher has pooled up several statements concerning to the problems of teachers working in private secondary schools after going through the literature available on the theme and after having discussions with the teachers working in private secondary schools.

The pooled up statements in the rating scale were rated in a three point scale, namely, Yes/Undecided/No. The preliminary rating scale was given to five teacher educators and ten private secondary school teachers to express their opinions on the scale. After getting their opinions on the scale, some of the statements were restated and some were deleted. A final scale with 35 statements was administered on a small sample of 15 teachers working in private secondary schools. The reliability of the test was found as 0.91 by following the split-half method and Spearman-Brown formula. So, it was considered as a final research tool.

The statements were in positive and negative form. The scores were given to them accordingly.

Administration of Tool

The rating scale was administered on a sample of 80 teachers working in private secondary schools of Vijayawada City.

4

Analysis of Data

The next step in the process of research, after the collection of data, is the organisation, analysis and interpretation of data and formulation of conclusions and generalisations to get a meaningful picture out of the raw information collected. The analysis and interpretation of data involve the objective material in the possession of the researcher and his subjective reactions and desires to be derived from the data.

The mass data collected through the use of questionnaire, need to be organised and systematized, i.e., edited, classified and tabulated before it can serve the purpose. Here, editing implies the checking of gathered data for accuracy, utility and completeness; classifying refers to the dividing of the information into different categories, classes or heads for use; and tabulating implies the recording of the classified material in accurate mathematical terms like making and counting frequency tallies for different items on which information is gathered.

Analysis of data means studying the tabulated material in order to determine inherent facts or meanings. In involves breaking down the existing complex factors into simpler parts and putting the parts together in new arrangements for purposes of interpretation.

The total score of teachers' problems of each teacher was taken to find out the difference in level of problems possessed by each sub-sample as well as total sample of the study. In the present study, the maximum score that a teacher can get is 105 and the minimum is 35. The highest score secured by a teacher was 98 and the lowest was 67.

The mean scores were used to identify the difference level of problems faced by private secondary teachers. The values of standard deviation were used to measure the spread or dispersion of scores in the distribution. The critical ratios were difference calculated to test the significant in the means of sub-samples of each variable and to accept or reject the hypothesis.

Hypothesis 1

"There are no problems to the private secondary school teachers".

To test the validity of hypothesis 1, the scores of all the private secondary school teachers were used to arrive at mean and standard deviation of the problems faced by the secondary school teachers working in private secondary schools.

Table—4.1 Problems of private secondary school teachers

Sample Size	*Mean*	*Standard Deviation*
80	85.69	1.54

As per the mean value seen in Table—4.1, the teachers working in private secondary schools of Vijayawada city were having several problems. As per the standard deviation value, the problems of private secondary school teachers were not scattered much.

The hypothesis that "there are no problems to the private secondary school teachers" can be rejected as there are several problems.

Hypothesis 2

There is no significant difference between the problems of men and women teachers working in private secondary schools".

To test the validity of hypothesis 2, the following calculations were made.

Table—4.2 Comparison of problems of men and women teachers

Variable	*Sample Size*	*Mean*	*S.D.*	*Mean Difference*	*Critical Ratio*
Male Teachers	40	84.87	7.65		
				1.63	0.95*
Female Teachers	40	86.50	7.68		

* not significant at 0.01 level

As per the values of Table—4.2, there was no significant difference between the problems of men and women teachers working in private secondary schools though they have several problems in the school and profession.

The hypothesis that "there is no significant difference between the problems of men and women teachers working in private secondary schools" can be accepted as there is no difference in their problems.

Hypothesis 3

"There is no significant difference between the problems of teachers working in recognised and unrecognised private secondary schools".

To test the validity of hypothesis 3, the following calculations were made.

As per the values of Table—4.3, there was no significant difference between the problems of teachers working in recognised and unrecognised private secondary schools though there were several problems. The little difference that existed may be due to technical errors.

Table—4.3 Comparison of problems of teachers working in recognised and unrecognised secondary schools

Variable	*Sample Size*	*Mean*	*S.D.*	*Mean Difference*	*Critical Ratio*
Unrecognised school teachers	34	83.67	8.13	3.5	2.2*
Recognised school teachers	46	87.17	7		

* not significant at 0.01 level

The hypothesis that "there is no significant difference between the problems of teachers working in recognised and unrecognised private secondary schools" can be accepted as there is no difference.

Hypothesis 4

"There is no significant difference between the problems of science and social studies teachers working in private secondary schools".

Table—4.4 Comparison of problems of science and social studies teachers

Variable	*Sample Size*	*Mean*	*S.D.*	*Mean Difference*	*Critical Ratio*
Science teachers	39	86.47	6.9	1.66	0.98*
Social studies teachers	41	84.81	8.35		

* not significant at 0.01 level

As per the values of Table—4.4, there was no significant difference between the problems of science and social studies teachers working in private secondary schools though there were several problems.

The hypothesis that "there is no significant difference between the problems of science and social studies teachers working in private secondary schools" can be accepted as there is no significant difference.

5

Summary, Conclusions and Discussions

A nation is built by its citizens, citizens are moulded by teachers and teachers are made by teacher educators. The National Policy on Education (1986) has rightly stated, "no people can rise above the level of its teachers". So, for the development of the country, it is very important to have good teachers and the good teachers can be produced only if we have a good system of teacher-education and efficient teacher educators. The success of an educational system largely depends upon the quality of teachers.

In ancient India, when the Gurukula system of education prevailed, the teacher was given the utmost respect in the society. But, the Indian teacher today finds himself in a new era entirely different from that of the teacher of the olden days. After independence and the establishment of democratic form of government, the teachers have a new set of ideas before them. It is the teacher that moulds the most precious material of the land, viz., the boys and girls, in their most impressionable periods of development into required shapes.

Choice of a job emerges as a result of the interplay of a multiplicity of factors. It is mainly the result of an interaction between factors pertaining to the job and those that characterise the chooser.

Teachers' problems involve pressures and aspirations connected with the profession. Every profession has got certain aspects conducive for job satisfaction. At the same time, it has other aspects which lead to create problems in their work. Teaching profession is no exception. If we find the solution of the problems, we can make them reduce.

Problems of teachers is a complex phenomenon involving various persona, academic, administrative, economic, institutional and social aspects. So, the researcher has a wider area in front of him. But, due to availability of the resources and permitted time, the researcher has limited this study only to private secondary school teachers of Vijayawada city. Of course, in this limited area also, few variables such as sex, subject and recognition status of the school have been taken into consideration.

A summary of the writings of recognised authorities and of previous research provides sufficient evidence that the research is familiar with what is already known and what is still unknown. It helps to eliminate duplication, to fix useful objectives, to form appropriate hypotheses, to draw meaningful conclusions and to make commendable suggestions. The options and suggestions about teaching staff given by the University Education Commission (1948), the Secondary Education Commission (1954) and the National Policy on Education (1986) were reviewed and mentioned. The works on problems of teachers of Ahmad (1984), Anjaneyulu (1968), Gangappa (1969), Srivastava (1979), Tali (1984), Trivedi (1961), Rawoot (1959), Philips (1965), Kumar (1982), Singh (1987), Passi and Sharma (1982), Santi Kumar (1961), Madhu (1978), Syama Sundara Rao (1971), Sommers (1969), David (1978), Nagapal (1972), etc., were cited.

Hence, the problem chosen for this study was an investigation into the problems of private secondary school teachers in relation to some variables. The variables considered in the study were sex, recognition status of the school, and teaching subject.

Objectives were identified keeping the different aspects of the present study in view. The main objectives of the study were:

1. To find out the problems of the private secondary school teachers;
2. To find out the problems of male and female teachers, private recognised and unrecognised school teachers, and science and social studies of private secondary schools.

Hypotheses were formulated taking the above objectives into consideration. The hypotheses were formulated in null form. The hypotheses of the present study were:

1. There are no problems to the private secondary school teachers;
2. There is no significant difference in the problems of men and women teachers, teachers of recognised and unrecognised schools, and science and social studies teachers.

Stratified sampling technique was found to be the most appropriate technique because the present study involved splitting of the sample into a good number of groups according to different variables. Through stratified sampling only it is possible to divide the sample into different groups and choose sample from each of these groups. Random sampling technique was also employed to select teachers from each group. Only the private secondary school teachers who teach science and social studies were included in the sample.

Regarding the size of the sample, 80 was found to be appropriate. This was found suitable because the study involved due intensity and detail, a sample with more than 80 teachers would involve lot of resources and less than 80 teachers would also bring about problem of representatives. Hence, 80 was considered to be suitable number for the sample. Out of the total sample, 40 teachers were male and 40 teachers were female. Regarding the recognition of schools, 34 teachers were from private unrecognised secondary schools and 46 teachers were from private recognised secondary schools. Regarding the teaching subject, 39 science teachers from private secondary schools and 41 social studies teachers from private secondary schools were selected.

The tools occupy a major role in any research study because they are useful in the collection and analysis of data and to draw meaningful conclusions. Construction and standardization of a good tool itself is a major research work. For this research work, a standardized tool was not available. So, the researcher constructed his own tool and used it to study the problems of private secondary school teachers.

For the purposes of analysis and drawing up of conclusions from the raw data, Mean, Standard Deviation and Critical Ratio were calculated.

Conclusions and Discussions

The following are the conclusions drawn from the present study on the problems of private secondary school teachers. The conclusions are analysed and discussed in order to utilise them in reducing the problems of private secondary school teachers.

1. The Teachers Working in Private Secondary Schools are Facing Several Problems.

The problems faced by the private secondary school teachers are concerned to the infrastructural facilities of the school, availability of audio-visual teaching aids, interference of management in teaching learning activities, decisions related to the disciplinary and indisciplinary activities of the students, respect given by the management and head of the institution to the teachers, payment of salaries based on qualifications and efficiency, honour given by the administrators to the opinion of the teachers, internal politics of the staff members, attitude of the head of the institution, implementation of innovative trends in teaching, requirement of inservice training, understanding of teachers about the teaching techniques, salaries of the staff, level and usefulness of the syllabus, strength of the students in a class, progress and disciplinary actions concerned to the individual students and their parents, teacher student relations, declination of moral values in teachers, family problems of the teachers, personality and health of the teachers, knowledge of the subject matter, getting status due to caste, religion and economic status rather than qualifications and efficiency in teaching, and satisfaction of the management.

As the teachers working in private secondary schools are having several problems, it is the obligation and responsibility of the government, management and other administrators to solve the above mentioned problems as far as possible in order to provide quality education to the clientele of these private schools. Otherwise, with dissatisfaction and frustration, the teachers working in these private schools will directly and or indirectly spoil the personality and career of the students. Similarly, the wastage that occurs in the classrooms of the teachers due to several administrative, personal and academic problems will result in the wastage of national and institutional material and manual resources along with the lives of blossoming buds. As the nation and society demand quality citizens with all required personality characteristics and the vocational skills, it is the duty of the teachers to impart quality instruction in their classrooms and to try to realise the goals of education. As the teachers have joined these schools on their own will and pleasure for the sake of employment, they have to strive for the upliftment of academic excellency in their classrooms rather than engaging in fault finding missions. The teachers with problems can approach the administrators and academicians to minimise or to avoid the problems as far as possible which are in their preview. Certain problems are unending and can never be solved as long as the classrooms continue on the land.

To do service to the child, it is the responsibility of the teacher to mould the child according to the requirement as the teacher has chosen the noblest profession of all professions of the mankind.

2. **The Men and Women Teachers Working in Private Secondary Schools are Facing Several Problems with No Difference.**

It is surprising to find that both men and women teachers are facing several problems with no significant difference though the personality and performance, needs and capabilities, attitudes and activities differ from one to the other significantly. Though there are several problems, both men and women teachers have to work for the benefit of their students.

3. **The Teachers Working in Unrecognised and Recognised Private Secondary Schools are Facing Several Problems Without any Significant Difference, Though the Teachers Working in Recognised Private Secondary Schools are having a Little Bit High Number of Problems Than Their Counterparts Working in Unrecognised Private Secondary Schools.**

The problems should be less in private recognised schools rather than in unrecognised private secondary schools as there will be some government interference in the management of recognised schools. But, to our surprise, the problems in the recognised schools are more when compared to their counterparts. This may be due to the gap between the administrators and the teachers and may also be regarding salary and such other aspects. Wherever the teachers may be working and whatever problems they may be facing, they must work for the common cause of education ignoring their tolerable problems.

4. **The Science and Social Studies Teachers Working in Private Secondary Schools are having Several Problems Without Any Significance Difference.**

Usually, in any school, the problems or the benefits will be common and it is seen here also. Both the science and social studies teachers should work well to provide better education by making their classrooms the temples of learning.

Suggestions for Further Research

The present study entitled "A study of the problems of private secondary school teachers" brings to light some of the areas to be investigated by taking research studies to identify and to solve the problems faced by teachers working in private schools.

1. Studies may be taken up taking other variables not studied in the present study.
2. Studies may be taken up to identify the problems taking a large sample from different levels of education.
3. Studies may be taken up to get possible solutions to the problems from the teachers itself.

Bibliography

Agarwal, J.C. (1985). *Theory and Principles of Education*. New Delhi: Vikas Publishing House Private Limited.

Anderson (1989). *The Effective Teacher*. New York: McGraw-Hill International Editions.

Best, J.W. and Kahn, J.V. (1989). *Research in Education*. New Delhi: Prentice-Hall of India Publishers Private Limited.

Bhatia and Bhatia (1997). *The Principles and Methods of Teaching*. New Delhi: Doaba House Book Sellers and Publishers.

Bhatnagar, S. (1992). *Indian Education Today and Tomorrow*. Meerut: International Publishing House.

Borg, R.W. and Gall (1963). *Educational Research*. New York and London: Longman.

Buch, M.B. *Third Survey of Educational Research*. New Delhi: National Council of Educational Research and Training.

Buch, M.B., Chief Editor. *Fourth Survey of Educational Research*, Vol. 2, New Delhi: National Council of Educational Research and Training.

Buch, M.B., Chief Editor. *Fifth Survey of Educational Research*, Vol. 1 New Delhi: National Council of Educational Research and Training.

Paul, K.P. (July, 1999). *"Who is a Good Teacher"*. The Educational Review 105 (7), pp. 18-19.

Goyal, J.C. (1985). *The Indian Teacher Educator, Some Characteristics*. Agra: National Psychological Corporation.

Grewal, P.S. (1990). *Methods of Statistical Analysis*. New Delhi: Sterling Publishers Private Limited.

Kochar, S.K. (1985). *Methods and Techniques of Teaching*. New Delhi: Sterling Publishers Private Limited.

Koul, L. (1984). *Methodology of Educational Research*. New Delhi: Vikas Publishing House Private Limited.

Kumar, A. (1991). *Current Trends in Indian Education*. New Delhi: Asish Publishing House.

Naidu, R.V. (1987). *Teacher's Behaviour and Students' Learning*. Hyderabad: Ramakrishna Press.

Pandey, R.S. (1983). *Principles of Education*. Agra: Vinod Pustak Mandir.

Prameela, A. (April, 2002). *"Teacher Education Current Issues and Restructuring Measures"*. Education Tracks. 1(7), pp: 23-25.

Rao, D.B., Editor (1988). *Teacher Education in India*. New Delhi: Discovery Publishing House.

Sharma, R.N. and R.K. (1983). *Research Methods in Social Sciences*. Bombay: Media Promoters and Publishers Private Limited.

Sidhu, K.S. (1990). *Methodology of Research in Education*. New Delhi: Sterling Publishers Private Limited.

Singh, A. (1995). *The Craft of Teaching*. New Delhi: Konark Publishers Private Limited.

Singh, R.P. (1984). *The Teachers in India*. New Delhi: National Publishing House.

Vijayalakshmi, G. (Feb, 2002), *"Factors Affecting Teacher Effectiveness"*. Edutracks. 1(5), p. 35.

Additional Reading

Bhaskara Rao, Digumarti (1994). *Scientific Aptitude*, New Delhi: Ashish Publishing House. ISBN 81-7024-658-X.

Bhaskara Rao, Digumarti (1995). *Animal Kingdom*. New Delhi: Discovery Publishing House. ISBN 81-7141-274-2.

Bhaskara Rao, Digumarti (1995). *Batracology*. New Delhi: Discovery Publishing House. ISBN 81-7141-279-3.

Bhaskara Rao, Digumarti (1997), *Scientific Attitude*. New Delhi: Discovery Publishing House. ISBN 81-7141-381-1.

Bhaskara Rao, Digumarti (1996). *Scientific Attitude vis-à-vis Scientific Aptitude*. New Delhi: Discovery Publishing House. ISBN 81-7141-308-0.

Bhaskara Rao, Digumarti (2004). *Scientific Attitude, Scientific Apitude and Achievement*, New Delhi: Discovery Publishing House.

Bhaskara Rao, Digumarti, Editor (1996). *Encyclopaedia of Education for All,* 5 Volumes. New Delhi: APH Publishing Corporation. ISBN 81-7024-759-4 (set).

Vol. I *Education for All: The World Conference*. ISBN 81-7024-760-8.

Vol. II *Education for All: The EPA-9 Summit*. ISBN 81-7024-761-6.

Vol. III *Education for All: Quality Education for All.* ISBN 81-7024-762-6.

Vol. IV *Education for All: Planning and Monitoring.* ISBN 81-7024-763-4.

Vol. V *Education for All: The Indian Scenario.* ISBN 81-7024-764-0.

Bhaskara Rao, Digumarti, Editor (1996). *Global Perceptions on Peace Education,* 3 Volumes. New Delhi: Discovery Publishing House. ISBN 81-7141-319-6.

Bhaskara Rao, Digumarti, Editor (1996). *National Policy on Education.* 2 Volumes. New Delhi: Anmol Publications Pvt. Ltd. ISBN 81-7488-323-1.

Bhaskara Rao, Digumarti, Editor (1997). *Care the Child,* 2 Volumes. New Delhi: Discovery Publishing House. ISBN 81-7141-394-3.

Bhaskara Rao, Digumarti, Editor (1997). *Education for the 21st Century.* New Delhi: Discovery Publishing House. ISBN 81-7141-389-7.

Bhaskara Rao, Digumarti, Editor (1997). *Reflections on Scientific Attitude.* New Delhi: Discovery Publishing House, ISBN 81-7141-319-6.

Bhaskara Rao, Digumarti, Editor (1997). *Success Story of a Primary Education Project.* New Delhi: APH Publishing Corporation. ISBN 81-7024-850-7.

Bhaskara Rao, Digumarti, Editor (1997). *World Food Summit.* New Delhi: Discovery Publishing House. ISBN 81-7141-386-2.

Bhaskara Rao, Digumarti, Editor (1998). *Adolescence Education.* New Delhi: Discovery Publishing House. ISBN 81-7141-432-X.

Bhaskara Rao, Digumarti, Editor (1998). *Community and School Nutrition Education.* New Delhi: Discovery Publishing House. ISBN 81-7141-435-4.

Bhaskara Rao, Digumarti, Editor (1998). *District Primary Education Programme.* New Delhi: Discovery Publishing House. ISBN 81-7141-396-X.

Bhaskara Rao, Digumarti, Editor (1998). *Earth Summit*, 2 Volumes. New Delhi: Discovery Publishing House. ISBN 81-7141-435-4.

Bhaskara Rao, Digumarti, Editor (1998). *National Policy on Education: Towards an Enlightened and Humane Society*, New Delhi: Discovery Publishing House. ISBN 81-7141-426-5.

Bhaskara Rao, Digumarti, Editor (1998). *Reforming School Education*. New Delhi: Discovery Publishing House. ISBN 81-7141-403-6.

Bhaskara Rao, Digumarti, Editor (1998). *Teacher Education in India*. New Delhi: Discovery Publishing House. ISBN 81-7141-406-[illegible]

Bhaskara Rao, Digumarti, Editor (1998). *World Summit for Social Development*. New Delhi: Discovery Publishing House. ISBN 81-7141-420-6.

Bhaskara Rao, Digumarti, Editor (2000). *Education for All: Achieving the Goal*, 3 Volumes, New Delhi: APH Publishing Corporation. ISBN 81-7648-152-1 (Set).

Vol. I *The Global Consensus*. ISBN 81-7648-155-6.

Vol. II *Mid-Decade Review Reports of Regional Seminars*. ISBN 81-7648-154-8.

Vol. III *Issues and Trends*. ISBN 81-7648-155-6.

Bhaskara Rao, Digumarti, Editor (1999), *International Encyclopaedia of AIDS*, 11 Volumes in 13 Parts. New Delhi: Discovery Publishing House. ISBN 81-7141-6 (Set).

Vol. 1 *Introduction to HIV/AIDS*. ISBN 81-7141-523-7.

Vol. 2 *HIV/AIDS—Issues and Challenges*, 2 Parts. ISBN 81-7141-524-5.

Vol. 3 *HIV/AIDS—Socio Economic Realities*. ISBN 81-7141-524-3.

Vol. 4 *HIV/AIDS—Law Ethics and Human Rights*, 2 Parts. ISBN 81-7141-526-1.

Vol. 5 *AIDS and NGOs*. ISBN 81-7141-527-X.

Vol. 6 *AIDS and Home Care*. ISBN 81-7141-528-8.

Vol. 7 *STD Case Management*. ISBN 81-7141-529-6.

Vol. 8 *HIV/AIDS Prevention and Care—Teaching Modules for Nurses and Midwives*. ISBN 81-7141-530-X.

Vol. 9 *HIV Prevention Education for Educational Institutions*. ISBN 81-7141-531-8.

Vol. 10 *Instructional Modules for AIDS Education*. ISBN 81-7141-532-6.

Vol. 11 *School Health Education to Prevent AIDS and STD—A Package for Curriculum Planners*. ISBN 81-7141-5338-4.

Bhaskara Rao, Digumarti, Editor (2000). *International Encyclopaedia of Science and Technology Education*, 11 Volumes. New Delhi: Discovery Publishing House. ISBN 81-7141-548-2 (Set).

Vol. 1 *Science and Technology Education*. ISBN 81-7141-568-7.

Vol. 2 *Science Education in Developing Countries*. ISBN 81-7141-570-9.

Vol. 3 *Organisational Structure of Science*. ISBN 81-7141-570-9.

Vol. 4 *Science Education in Asia and the Pacific*. ISBN 81-7141-571-7.

Vol. 5 *Science and Technology Education for All*. ISBN 81-7141-572-5.

Vol. 6 *Values, Ethics, Talent and Girls in Science and Technology Education*. ISBN 81-7141-573-3.

Vol. 7 *Popularization of Science and Technology Education*. ISBN 81-7141-574-1.

Vol. 8 *Science, Power and Society*. ISBN 81-7141-575-X.

Vol. 9 *Information Technology*. ISBN 81-7141-576-8.

Vol. 10 *Teacher Training in Science and Technology Education*. ISBN 81-7141-577-6.

Vol. 11 *Teacher Training in Science and Technology: A Curriculum Framework*. ISBN 81-7141-578-4.

Bhaskara Rao, Digumarti, Editor (2001). *Distance Education in Different Countries*. New Delhi: APH Publishing Corporation. ISBN 81-7648-229-3.

Bhaskara Rao, Digumarti, Editor (2001). *Decentralised Management of Education (Management of Education in Panchayati Raj and Municipal Bodies)*. New Delhi: Discovery Publishing House. ISBN 81-7141-617-9.

Bhaskara Rao, Digumarti, Editor (2001). *Electrochemistry for Environmental Protection*. New Delhi: Discovery Publishing House. ISBN 81-7141-619-5.

Bhaskara Rao, Digumarti, Editor (2001). *Global Educational Studies*. New Delhi: Discovery Publishing House. ISBN 81-7141-616-0.

Bhaskara Rao, Digumarti, Editor (2001). *Global Synthesis of Educational Assessment*. New Delhi: Discovery Publishing House. ISBN 81-7141-613-6.

Bhaskara Rao, Digumarti, Editor (2000). *International Encyclopaedia of Human Rights*. 7 Volumes in 13 Parts. New Delhi: Discovery Publishing House. (Royal Size). ISBN 81-7141-567-9 (Set).

Vol. 1 *International Instruments of Human Rights*, 2 Parts. ISBN 81-7141-595-4.

Vol. 2 *Regional Instruments of Human Rights*. ISBN 81-7141-604-7.

Vol. 3 *Human Rights and the United Nations*, 2 Parts. ISBN 81-7141-605-5.

Vol. 4 *Fact Files of Human Rights*, 3 Parts. ISBN 81-7141-605-3.

Vol. 5 *Study Stories of Human Rights*, 3 Parts. ISBN 81-7141-607-3.

Vol. 6 *International Meetings on Human Rights*, 2 Parts. ISBN 81-7141-608-X.

Vol. 7 *Professional Training in Human Rights*. ISBN 81-7141-609-8.

Bhaskara Rao, Digumarti, Editor (2001). *Jomtein Decade of Education*. New Delhi: Discovery Publishing House. ISBN 81-7141-618-7.

Bhaskara Rao, Digumarti, Editor (2001). *Nuclear Materials: Issues and Concerns*, 2 Volumes. New Delhi: Discovery Publishing House. ISBN 81-7141-611-X.

Bhaskara Rao, Digumarti, Editor (2001). *World Conference on Education for All*. New Delhi: APH Publishing Corporation. ISBN 81-7141-274-9.

Bhaskara Rao, Digumarti, Editor (2001). *World Conference on Higher Education*, New Delhi: Discovery Publishing House. ISBN 81-7141-610-1.

Bhaskara Rao, Digumarti, Editor (2001). *World Conference on Science*. New Delhi: Discovery Publishing House. ISBN 81-7141-612-8.

Bhaskara Rao, Digumarti, Editor (2003). *Inspiring Experiences in Teacher Education*. New Delhi: Discovery Publishing House. ISBN 81-7141-656-X.

Bhaskara Rao, Digumarti, Editor (2003). *International Studies in Education*, 3 Volumes, New Delhi: Discovery Publishing House. ISBN 81-7141-647-0.

Bhaskara Rao, Digumarti, Editor (2003). *Military Conversion: Impact on Science and Technology*, New Delhi: Discovery Publishing House. ISBN 81-7141-578-4.

Bhaskara Rao, Digumarti, Editor (2003). *United Nations Millennium Summit*. New Delhi: Discovery Publishing House. ISBN 81-7141-632-2.

Bhaskara Rao, Digumarti, Editor (2003). *World Assembly on Aging*. New Delhi: Discovery Publishing House. ISBN 81-7141-637-3.

Bhaskara Rao, Digumarti, Editor (2003). *World Conference on Human Rights*. New Delhi: Discovery Publishing House. ISBN 81-7141-661-6.

Bhaskara Rao, Digumarti, Editor (2003). *World Education Forum*. New Delhi: Discovery Publishing House. ISBN 81-7141-639-X.

Bhaskara Rao, Digumarti, Editor (2003). *Education Employment and Human Resource Development.* New Delhi: Discovery Publishing House. ISBN 81-7141-681-0.

Bhaskara Rao, Digumarti, Editor (2003). *Successful Schooling.* New Delhi: Discovery Publishing House. ISBN 81-7141-677-2.

Bhaskara Rao, Digumarti, Editor (2003). *European Education and Teachers.* New Delhi: Discovery Publishing House. ISBN 81-7141-702-7.

Bhaskara Rao, Digumarti, Editor (2003). *Teachers in a Changing World.* New Delhi: Discovery Publishing House. ISBN 81-7141-694-2.

Bhaskara Rao, Digumarti, Editor (2004). *Learning to Live Together*, 4 Volumes. New Delhi: Discovery Publishing House.

- Vol. 1 *International Conference on Learning to Live Together.*
- Vol. 2 *Globalisation and Living Together.*
- Vol. 3 *Curriculum for Learning to Live Together.*
- Vol. 4 *Science Education for the Contemporary Society.*

Bhaskara Rao, Digumarti, Editor (2004). *International Guidelines on Open and Distance Teacher Education*, New Delhi: Discovery Publishing House.

Bhaskara Rao Digumarti, Editor (2004). *Adult Learning in the 21st Century*, New Delhi: Discovery Publishing House.

Bhaskara Rao, Digumarti, Editor (2004). *Educational Practices: Research and Recommendations.* New Delhi: Discovery Publishing House.

Bhaskara Rao, Digumarti, Editor (2004). *Chernobyl: Never Again.* New Delhi: APH Publishing Corporation.

Bhaskara Rao, Digumarti, Editor (2004). *Virology and Immunology.* New Delhi: APH Publishing Corporation.

Bhaskara Rao, Digumarti, C.A.P. Swamy and B.S.V. Dutt (1997). *Self-Evaluation in Student Teaching.* New Delhi: Discovery Publishing House. ISBN 81-7141-374-9.

Bhaskara Rao, Digumarti and B.S.V. Dutt, Editors (2003). *Education: Programmes and Policies*. New Delhi: APH Publishing Corporation. ISBN 81-7648-470-9.

Bhaskara Rao, Digumarti and D. Naresh Kumar (2004). *School Teacher Effectiveness*. New Delhi: Discovery Publishing House.

Bhaskara Rao, Digumarti and D. Sridhar (2002). *Job Satisfaction of School Teachers*. New Delhi: Discovery Publishing House. ISBN 81-7141-652-7.

Bhaskara Rao, Digumarti and Digumarti Pushpa Latha (1994). *Achievement in Biology*. New Delhi: Discovery Publishing House. ISBN 81-7141-264-5.

Bhaskara Rao, Digumarti, C. Sridevi and K. Vijaya (1995). *Achievement in Social Studies*. New Delhi: Discovery Publishing House. ISBN 81-7141-281-5.

Bhaskara Rao, Digumarti and Digumarti Pushpa Latha (1995). *Achievement in English*. New Delhi: Discovery Publishing House. ISBN 81-7141-283-1.

Bhaskara Rao, Digumarti and Digumarti Pushpa Latha (1994). *Achievement in Science*. New Delhi: Discovery Publishing House. ISBN 81-7141-280-70.

Bhaskara Rao, Digumarti and Digumarti Pushpa Latha (1995). *Achievement in Mathematics*. New Delhi: Discovery Publishing House. ISBN 81-7141-278-5.

Bhaskara Rao, Digumarti and Digumarti Pushpa Latha, Editors (1998). *International Encyclopaedia of Women*. 5 Volumes. New Delhi: Discovery Publishing House. ISBN 81-7141-410-9 (Set).

Vol. 1 *Status of World's Women*. ISBN 81-7141-494-X.

Vol. 2 *Women, Education and Empowerment*. ISBN 81-7141-498-1.

Vol. 3 *Women Challenges and Advancement*. ISBN 81-7141-497-4.

Vol. 4 *Women and Family Health*. ISBN 81-7141-497-4.

Vol. 5 *Women and International Action*. ISBN 81-7141-498-2.

Bhaskara Rao, Digumarti, Digumarti Pushpa Latha and Digumarti Harshitha, Editors (2001). *Biological Warfare*. New Delhi: Discovery Publishing House. ISBN 81-7141-597-0.

Bhaskara Rao, Digumarti, Digumarti Pushpa Latha and Digumarti Harshitha, Editors (2001). *Women as Educators*. New Delhi: Discovery Publishing House. ISBN 81-7141-602-0.

Bhaskara Rao, Digumarti and Digumarti Harshitha, Editors (2001). *Education in India*. New Delhi: APH Publishing Corporation. ISBN 81-7141-207-2.

Bhaskara Rao, Digumarti, Digumarti Pushpa Latha and Digumarti Harshitha, Editors (2001). *Assessing Learning Achievement*. New Delhi: Discovery Publishing House. ISBN 81-7141-601-2.

Bhaskara Rao, Digumarti, Digumarti Pushpa Latha and Digumarti Harshitha, Editors (2001). *Energy Security*. New Delhi: Discovery Publishing House. ISBN 81-7141-598-9.

Bhaskara Rao, Digumarti, Digumarti Harshitha and K.R.S.S. Rao, Editors (1999). *Advanced Biotechnology*. New Delhi: Discovery Publishing House. ISBN 81-7141-516-4.

Bhaskara Rao, Digumarti and K.R.S. Sambhasiva Rao, Editors (1996). *Current Trends in Indian Education*. New Delhi: Discovery Publishing House. ISBN 81-7141-311-0.

Bhaskara Rao, Digumarti and K. Vijaya (1995). *A Text Book of Evaluation*. Ambala Cantt: The Associated Publishers.

Bhaskara Rao, Digumarti and N.V.M. Mohana Rao (2002). *Problems of Mentally Handicapped Children*. New Delhi: Discovery Publishing House. ISBN 81-7141-645-4.

Bhaskara Rao, Digumarti and S. Chandra Mohan (2002). *Sports Management*. New Delhi: APH Publishing Corporation. ISBN 81-7648-467-9.

Bhaskara Rao, Digumarti and Sk. Johni Basha (2004). *Teachers' Population Education Awareness*. New Delhi: APH Publishing Corporation.

Bhaskara Rao, Digumarti, V.V. Rao, Lakshmi and V.V. Krishna, Editors (1999). *Status and Advancement of Women*. New Delhi: APH Publishing Corporation. ISBN 81-7648-169-6.

Babu, P.C., Author and Digumarti Bhaskara Rao, Editor (2004). *Flowers of Wisdom*. New Delhi: Discovery Publishing House. ISBN 81-7141-695-0.

Bhagya Lakshmi, Lingineni, Author and Digumarti Bhaskara Rao, Editor (2000). *Reading and Comprehension*. New Delhi: Discovery Publishing House. ISBN 81-7141-543-1.

Bhuvaneswara Lakshmi, Gadde, Author and Digumarti Bhaskara Rao, Editor (2000). *Attitude Towards Science*. New Delhi: Discovery Publishing House. ISBN 81-7141-541-6.

Devraj, T.A.S., Author and Digumarti Bhaskara Rao, Editor (1997). *Trace Analysis of Uranium and Thorium*. New Delhi: Discovery Publishing House. ISBN 81-7141-375-7.

Durga Rani, K., Author and Digumarti Bhaskara Rao, Editor (2000). *Educational Aspirations and Scientific Attitudes*. New Delhi: Discovery Publishing House. ISBN 81-7141-555-55.

Dutt, B.S.V., and Digumarti Bhaskara Rao (2001). *Empowering Primary Teachers*. New Delhi: Discovery Publishing House. ISBN 81-7141-615-2.

Ediger, Marlow and Digumarti Bhaskara Rao (1996). *Science Curriculum*. New Delhi: Discovery Publishing House. ISBN 81-7141-321-8.

Ediger, Marlow and Digumarti Bhaskara Rao (2000). *Teaching Mathematics Successfully*. New Delhi: Discovery Publishing House. ISBN 81-7141-552-0.

Ediger, Marlow and Digumarti Bhaskara Rao (2001). *Teaching Science Successfully*. New Delhi: Discovery Publishing House. ISBN 81-7141-600-4.

Ediger, Marlow and Digumarti Bhaskara Rao (2001). *Teaching Social Studies Successfully*. New Delhi: Discovery Publishing House. ISBN 81-7141-596-2.

Ediger, Marlow and Digumarti Bhaskara Rao (2002). *Philosophy and Curriculum*. New Delhi: Discovery Publishing House. ISBN 81-7141-631-4.

Ediger, Marlow and Digumarti Bhaskara Rao (2002). *Improving School Administration*. New Delhi: Discovery Publishing House. ISBN 81-7141-633-0.

Ediger, Marlow and Digumarti Bhaskara Rao (2002). *Elementary Curriculum*. New Delhi: Discovery Publishing House. ISBN 81-7141-658-6.

Ediger, Marlow and Digumarti Bhaskara Rao (2003). *Language Arts Curriculum*. New Delhi: Discovery Publishing House. ISBN 81-7141-657-8.

Ediger, Marlow and Digumarti Bhaskara Rao (2003). *Psychology and Curriculum*. New Delhi: Discovery Publishing House. ISBN 81-7141-691-8.

Ediger, Marlow and Digumarti Bhaskara Rao (2003). *Teaching Language Arts Successfully*. New Delhi: Discovery Publishing House. ISBN 81-7141-678-0.

Ediger, Marlow and Digumarti Bhaskara Rao (2003). *School Curriculum and Administration*. New Delhi: Discovery Publishing House. ISBN 81-7141-709-4.

Ediger, Marlow and Digumarti Bhaskara Rao (2003). *Teaching Mathematics in Elementary Schools*. New Delhi: Discovery Publishing House. ISBN 81-7141-687-X.

Ediger, Marlow and Digumarti Bhaskara Rao (2003). *Teaching Science in Elementary Schools*. New Delhi: Discovery Publishing House. ISBN 81-7141-698-5.

Ediger, Marlow and Digumarti Bhaskara Rao (2003). *School Curriculum and Administration*. New Delhi: Discovery Publishing House. ISBN 81-7141-709-4.

Ediger, Marlow and Digumarti Bhaskara Rao (2003). *Elementary Curriculum Improvement*. New Delhi: Discovery Publishing House. ISBN 81-7141-740-X.

Ediger, Marlow and Digumarti Bhaskara Rao (2004). *Modern Elementary School*. New Delhi: Discovery Publishing House.

Ediger, Marlow and Digumarti Bhaskara Rao (2004). *Relevancy in Elementary Curriculum*, New Delhi: Discovery Publishing House.

Ediger, Marlow and Digumarti Bhaskara Rao, (2004). *Teaching Social Studies in Elementary Schools*. New Delhi: Discovery Publishing House.

Ediger Marlow, B.S.V. Dutt and Digumarti Bhaskara Rao (2003). *Teaching English Successfully*. New Delhi: Discovery Publishing House. ISBN 81-7141-707-8.

Harshitha, Digumarti and Digumarti Bhaskara Rao, Editors (2004). *Educational Innovations in Action*. New Delhi: Discovery Publishing House.

Indira Devi, Author and J. Prasanth Kumar and Digumarti Bhaskara Rao, Editors (2004). *Values in Language Text Books*. New Delhi: Discovery Publishing House.

Jayasree, Kandi, Author and Digumarti Bhaskara Rao, Editor (1999). *Correlates of Socialisation*. New Delhi: Discovery Publishing House. ISBN 81-7141-517-2.

John Babu, Chikati, Author and T.J.R. Prasad, G.M. Madhukar and Digumarti Bhaskara Rao, Editors (1996). *Problem Solving in Mathematics*. New Delhi: APH Publishing Corporation. ISBN 81-7648-273-0.

Lalitha, T., Author and K.S. Prabhakaram, D.S.N. Sastry and Digumarti Bhaskara Rao, Editors (2004). *Educational Philosophic Beliefs*. New Delhi: Discovery Publishing House.

Madhu Bala, Jampala, Author and Digumarti Bhaskara Rao, Editor (2004). *Adjustment Problems of Hearing Impaired*. New Delhi: Discovery Publishing House.

Marja, Talvi and Digumarti Bhaskara Rao, Editors (1996). *Educational Leadership and Social Changes*. New Delhi: Discovery Publishing House. ISBN 81-7141-320-X.

Nirmala Jyothi, M., Author and Digumarti Bhaskara Rao, Editor (2003). *Non-detention Systems in School Education*. New Delhi: Discovery Publishing House. ISBN 81-7141-654-3.

Prabhakaram, K.S., Author and Digumarti Bhaskara Rao, Editor (1998). *Concept Attainment Model in Mathematics Teaching*. New Delhi: Discovery Publishing House. ISBN 81-7141-424-9.

Prasanth Kumar, J., Author and Digumarti Bhaskara Rao, Editor (1998). *Effectiveness of Distance Education System*. New Delhi: Discovery Publishing House. ISBN 81-7141-437-0.

Prasanth Kumar, J., Author and G. Sundara Rao and Digumarti Bhaskara Rao, Editors (2000). *Open University Student Support Services*. New Delhi: Discovery Publishing House. ISBN 81-7141-550-4.

Ramatulasamma, K., Author and Digumarti Bhaskara Rao, Editor (2002). *Job Satisfaction of Teacher Educators*, New Delhi: Discovery Publishing House. ISBN 81-7141-655-1.

Rama Krishnaiah, D., Author and Digumarti Bhaskara Rao, Editor (1998). *Job Satisfaction of College Teachers*, New Delhi: Discovery Publishing House. ISBN 81-7141-438-9.

Rama Kumar Ratnam, M., Author and Digumarti Bhaskara Rao, Editor (1998). *Dukha: Suffering in Early Buddhism*. New Delhi: Discovery Publishing House. ISBN 81-7141-653-5.

Rathaiah, Lavu and Digumarti Bhaskara Rao, Editors (1996). *International Innovations in Education*. New Delhi: Discovery Publishing House. ISBN 81-7141-359-5.

Ramesh, Ganta and Digumarti Bhaskara Rao, Editors (1998). *Environmental Education: Problems and Prospects*. New Delhi: Discovery Publishing House. ISBN 81-7141-423-0.

Rathaiah, Lavu and Digumarti Bhaskara Rao (1997). *Achievement Correlates*. New Delhi: Discovery Publishing House. ISBN 81-7141-385-4.

Reddy, Sudhakar Y., Author, and Digumarti Bhaskara Rao, Editor (2003). *Creativity in Adolescents*. New Delhi: Discovery Publishing House. ISBN 81-7141-659-4.

Reddy, M.S., Author and Digumarti Bhaskara Rao, Editor (2004). *Creativity in College Students*. New Delhi: Discovery Publishing House. ISBN 81-7141-697-7.

Radramamba, B., Author and Digumarti Bhaskara Rao, Editor (2003). *Problems of Teaching*. New Delhi: APH Publishing Corporation. ISBN 81-7648-462-8.

Sanjeeva Rao, P.C., Author and Digumarti Bhaskara Rao, Editor (1996). *A Text Book of Geology*. New Delhi: Discovery Publishing House. ISBN 81-7141-313-7.

Satya Narayana V., Author and Digumarti Bhaskara Rao, Editor (2001). *Physical Education, Social Attitudes and Leadership Qualities*. New Delhi: Discovery Publishing House. ISBN 81-7141-593-8.

Srinivasulu Reddy, M., and K.R.S. Sambasiva Rao, Authors and Digumarti Bhaskara Rao, Editor (1999). *A Text Book of Aquaculture*. New Delhi: Discovery Publishing House. ISBN 81-7141-482-6.

Srinivasa Rao, Mandalapu, Author and Digumarti Bhaskara Rao, Editor (2003). *Achievement Motivation and Achievement in Mathematics*. New Delhi: Discovery Publishing House. ISBN 81-7141-674-8.

Vanaja, M. Author and Digumarti Bhaskara Rao, Editor (1999). *Inquiry Training Model*. New Delhi: Discovery Publishing House. ISBN 81-7141-515-6.

Vanaja. M. and N. Sneha Latha, Authors and Digumarti Bhaskara Rao, Editor (2004). *Student Shyness*. New Delhi: APH Publishing Corporation.

Valeri V. Koustiouk, Author and Digumarti Bhaskara Rao, Editor (2002). *A Text Book of Cryogenics*. New Delhi: Discovery Publishing House. ISBN 81-7141-642-X.

Valeri V. Koustiouk, Author and Digumarti Bhaskara Rao, Editor (2004). *Refrigeration and Environment*. New Delhi: APH Publishing Corporation.

Veena Kumari, Balusu and Digumarti Bhaskara Rao (1996). *Operation Black Board*. New Delhi: APH Publishing Corporation. ISBN 81-7024-711-X.

Veena Kumari, Balusu, Author and Digumarti Bhaskara Rao, Editor (2000). *Psycho-Social Correlates of Achievement*, New Delhi: Discovery Publishing House. ISBN 81-7141-547-4.

Venkata Rao, P. and Digumarti Bhaskara Rao (1989). *A Text Book of Zoology—Junior Intermediate*. Guntur: Vignan Publishers.

Venkata Rao, P. and Digumarti Bhaskara Rao (1989). *A Text Book of Zoology—Senior Intermediate*. Guntur: Vignan Publishers.

Venugopala Rao, K., Author and Digumarti Bhaskara Rao, Editor (2000). *Teacher Morale in Secondary Schools*. New Delhi: Discovery Publishing House. ISBN 81-7141-551-2.

Vidya, C., Author and Digumarti Bhaskara Rao. Editor (1996). *A Text Book of Nutrition*. New Delhi: Discovery Publishing House. ISBN 81-7141-309-9.

Vidya Bharathi, D., Author and Digumarti Bhaskara Rao, Editor (2000). *Educational Philosophies of Swami Vivekananda and John Dewey*. New Delhi: APH Publishing Corporation. ISBN 81-7648-309-9.

Books in Telugu Language

Bhaskara Rao, Digumarti (1986). *Dhrushya Sravana Bodhanapakaranalu* (Audio Visual Teaching Aids). Guntur: Sri Nagarjuna Publishers.

Bhaskara Rao, Digumarti (1993). *Jeevasashtra Bodhana* (Teaching of Biology). Guntur: Sri Nagarjuna Publishers.

Bhaskara Rao, Digumarti (1995). *Vignanasasthra Bodhana* (Teaching of Science) Guntur: Sri Nagarjuna Publishers.

Bhaskara Rao, Digumarti (1997). *Vidya Manovignana Seshtram* (Educational Psychology). Guntur: Creative Press.

Bhaskara Rao, Digumarti (1998). *DSC Study Material*. Guntur: Sri Nagarjuna Publishers.

Bhaskara Rao, Digumarti (1998). *Upadhyayudu Vidya*. (Teacher and Education). Guntur: Sri Nagarjuna Publishers.

Bhaskara Rao, Digumarti (1998). *Vidya Drukpadalu* (Prespectives of Education). Guntur: Sri Nagarjuna Publishers.

Bhaskara Rao, Digumarti (1999). *EdCET Teaching Aptitude*. Guntur: Sri Nagarjuna Publishers.

Bhaskara Rao, Digumarti (2001). *Bharata Samajamulo Upadyayudu Vidya* (Teacher and Education in Emerging Indian Society). Guntur: Sri Nagarjuna Publishers.

Bhaskara Rao, Digumarti (2001). *Bhoutika Sastra Bodhana Paddathulu* (Methods of Teaching Physical Science). Guntur: Sri Nagarjuna Publishers.

Bhaskara Rao, Digumarti (2001). *Jeeva Sastra Bodhana Padhathulu* (Methods of Teaching Biology). Guntur: Nagarjuna Publishers.

Bhaskara Rao, Digumarti (2001). *Vidya Manovignana Sastram* (Educational Psychology). Guntur: Sri Nagarjuna Publishers.

Bhaskara Rao, Digumarti (2003). *Patsala Yajamanyam / Paripalana* (School Management and Administration). Guntur: Sri Nagarjuna Publishers.

Bhaskara Rao, Digumarti (2004). *Vidya Sanketika Sastram mariyu Computer Vidya* (Educational Technology and Computer Education). Guntur: Sri Nagarjuna Publishers.

Appendix

Problems of Private Secondary School Teachers

Respected Teachers,

Please put (✓) mark on Yes or Undecided or No given against each statement. Your frank and free opinions will help in drawing out real problems and to find solutions to teachers' problems. Your responses will be kept confidential and used only for research purpose.

Thanking you,

Yours sincerely,

Researcher

Name .... Qualification ....

Age .... Experience ....

Subject .... Designation ....

School ....

1. In our school, we have the required Teaching Learning Material — Yes/Undecided/No
2. I think that, in our school, we have more working hours. — Yes/Undecided/No
3. I am satisfied with the way problems of teachers are solved. — Yes/Undecided/No
4. I have full freedom regarding teaching in our school. — Yes/Undecided/No

5.	In our school, we get recognition and respect for hard work.	Yes/Undecided/No
6.	I feel, there is job security in our school.	Yes/Undecided/No
7.	I think my views regarding the teaching strategies for the development of school are valued.	Yes/Undecided/No
8.	Our school correspondent takes action about our welfare.	Yes/Undecided/No
9.	I am allotted study hours in addition to the school teaching hours.	Yes/Undecided/No
10.	There is interference of the correspondent in the teaching duties.	Yes/Undecided/No
11.	My Head Master co-operates with me when the student is punished for his mistake.	Yes/Undecided/No
12.	My correspondent appreciates my hard work and good results in my subject.	Yes/Undecided/No
13.	I think the salaries are given according to the ability and qualification.	Yes/Undecided/No
14.	Inservice training is provided in new methods of teaching in our school.	Yes/Undecided/No
15.	I face problems because of internal politics between the teachers of our school.	Yes/Undecided/No
16.	I face problems because of the attitude of the Head Master.	Yes/Undecided/No
17.	I think my teaching is according to the mental levels of the pupils.	Yes/Undecided/No
18.	The present syllabus is suitable for the teachers to teach.	Yes/Undecided/No
19.	Due to the lack of understanding about teaching methods, I am unable to teach properly.	Yes/Undecided/No
20.	I face problems from meritorious students as I do not possess up-to-date knowledge.	Yes/Undecided/No
21.	When I get doubt about teaching any lesson, I discuss with my colleagues and clear my doubt.	Yes/Undecided/No

22.	I face problems of indiscipline from students of high socio economic status.	Yes/Undecided/No
23.	I face problems while teaching because of over crowded class.	Yes/Undecided/No
24.	I face problems of from parents regarding progress reports and the punishments measured out to them.	Yes/Undecided/No
25.	I face problems of indiscipline because of the deteriorating relationship between teacher and students.	Yes/Undecided/No
26.	I think, in our institution, salaries are not paid according to qualification and ability.	Yes/Undecided/No
27.	I think, because of the deterioration of moral values in the teachers, the students are disobedient and give rise to problems.	Yes/Undecided/No
28.	I think family problems are obstacles in my classroom teaching.	Yes/Undecided/No
29.	I feel inconvenient because I lack the skill to move freely and have good relationship with others.	Yes/Undecided/No
30.	I think because of the working hours allotted me, I get tired and am unable to teach properly.	Yes/Undecided/No
31.	I think, we get recognition and honour because of teaching skill, but not based on caste, religion and economic status.	Yes/Undecided/No
32.	I think I have teaching ability as well as good administrative skill.	Yes/Undecided/No
33.	I think our correspondent is satisfied with my conduct.	Yes/Undecided/No
34.	Health problems influence my teaching.	Yes/Undecided/No
35.	I support teaching lessons using methods of teaching.	Yes/Undecided/No

Index

A

Administration of Tool, 36
Age and Teachers' Problems, 22
Anjaneyulu, 24

B

Brahman, 2
Buddhist period, 3

C

California Institute of Technology (1953-54), 24
Carr-Saunders, A.M., 6
Commonwealth Confrence (1974), 18,19

D

David, John, 26
Dewey, 1

E

Economic Status and Teachers' Problems, 21-22
Education as a protector, 5
– Commission (1964-66), 18
– for all, 5
Efficiency and teacher's problems, 24-25
Experience and teachers' problems, 23

F

Facilities and teachers problems, 25-26
Fee, 7
Film starips, 23

G

Gavelhi, 1
Guru, 2,8
Gurukula, 2

H

Hypotheses of the study, 30-31

I

Importance of education in human life, 4-5
Islam, 3

J

Jewelt, 25
Job satisfaction and teachers' problems, 20-21

K

Knowledge, 13, 14, 17
Koran, 3
Kumar, Shanti, 23

L

Language and non-language teacher's problem, 23-24

Learning in India, 2

M

Madhu, V., 23, 25
Mammon worship, 6
Management and teacher's problems, 24
Manual skill, 3
Marital status and teachers problems, 26
Men and women teachers, 29
Military science, 3
Mudaliar Commission, 16,17
Muslim, 3

N

Nagpal, G.L., 26
National Policy on Education, 5
Nature of teaching, 18
Need of the study, 11-12
Newson Committee, 17
Norwood report, 17

O

Operational definitions of key terms, 27

P

Passi, 22
Philips, 22
Postalozzi, 4
Private schools, 27-28

R

Rajagopalan, S., 9
Rao, Syama Sundra, 24,26
Rawoot, 22
Recognised and unrecognised school teachers, 30
Role of the teacher, 18-20
Ryburn, 18

S

Salary, 7
Science and scocial studies teachers, 30
Scope of the study, 12
Secondary Education Commission, 5, 14-17
– School Teachers, 29
Sex and teacher's problems, 22-23
Singh V.P., 23
Singh, U.P., 22
Socrate, 1
Spens report, 17
Srivastava, U., 22, 23, 26
Srivastava, V., 21
Statement of the problem, 11

T

Tagore, 8
Tali, R. 21, 24, 25
Teacher, 7-11, 28-29
– effectiveness, 20
Teaching, 6-7
– profession, 9
Thomas, F.W. 2
Trivedi, K.P., 21, 24, 25

U

Universalisation of elementary education, 5

V

Variables of the study, 29
Vedic period, 2

Y

Yagnavalka, 1